KNOWLEDGE AND THE BODY–MIND PROBLEM

KNOWLEDGE AND THE BODY–MIND PROBLEM

In defence of interaction

Karl R. Popper

Edited by
M.A. Notturno

London and New York

First published 1994
by Routledge
11 New Fetter Lane, London EC4P 4EE

Simultaneously published in the USA and Canada
by Routledge
29 West 35th Street, New York, NY 10001

Typeset in Garamond by Solidus (Bristol) Limited
Printed and bound in Great Britain by
TJ Press Ltd, Padstow, Cornwall

British Library Cataloguing in Publication Data
A catalogue record for this book is available from the
British Library

Library of Congress Cataloging in Publication Data
Popper, Karl Raimund, Sir
Knowledge and the body–mind problem: in defence of interaction/
Karl Popper: edited by M.A. Notturno.
p.   cm.
Based upon lectures delivered by the author at Emory University in 1969.
Includes bibliographical references and indexes.
1. Mind and body.   2. Knowledge, Theory of.   I. Notturno, Mark
Amadeus.   II.   Title.
BF161.P584   1994
128'.2–dc20   94–14610

ISBN 0–415–11504–3

To Melitta

CONTENTS

ACKNOWLEDGEMENTS

This volume is the second to have been compiled from my papers deposited with the Hoover Institution at Stanford, California. I am once again greatly indebted to my friend Dr Werner Baumgartner and the Ianus Foundation for enabling Dr Mark Notturno and his wife Kira to edit and thoroughly revise these lectures. I thank them both for their hard work and tireless application to this difficult task. Raymond Mew and my assistant Melitta Mew have made important suggestions in connection with the text, and have kept me alive while I was trying to oversee its production.

K.R.P.
Kenley, 17 March 1994

AUTHOR'S NOTE, 1993

The following chapters are based upon lectures that I delivered at Emory University in 1969 on the body–mind problem. In them, I suggest a theory of mind–body interaction that I relate to evolutionary emergence, human language, and what I have, since the mid-1960s, called 'world 3'. In order to present the theory, it is necessary to proceed systematically and to introduce you to some of the ideas that I use in the presentation of the theory itself. These are, notably, the ideas of subjective and objective knowledge; the theory of the 'three worlds'; and something about evolution, emergence, and the functions of language. A presentation of these will take up the first few chapters. While I have extensively revised the lectures as they were given, I have decided to retain the lecture format in order to make for easy readability. The original lectures were followed by discussion. I have tried to incorporate parts of this in my lectures where appropriate, and have taken the rest of it, where relevant, as appendixes to the lectures.

These lectures, as you will soon see, deviate somewhat from what I had originally planned, and from what I originally announced. This is because I changed my plan for the lectures when it became apparent, during the first discussion, and in the informal discussions afterwards, that my audience was very interested in my world 3. World 3 is, in any event, a crucial part of my approach to the body–mind problem, and my thesis, in a nutshell, can be put as follows: in order to understand the relationship between the body and the mind, we must first recognize the existence of objective knowledge as an objective and autonomous product of the human mind, and, in particular, the ways in which we use such knowledge as a control system for critical problem-solving.

K.R.P.
Kenley, 1993

1

KNOWLEDGE:
OBJECTIVE AND
SUBJECTIVE

Ladies and Gentlemen:

It is a great honour to be invited to Emory, and I am very conscious of the fact that this invitation has put a great burden of responsibility on my shoulders. I have called this series of lectures 'Knowledge and the Body–Mind Problem'. I should perhaps have given it a better-sounding title, like: 'Human Knowledge and the Human Mind'. But this sounds a little airy, and I am allergic to hot air – even more than to tobacco smoke.

I have planned these six lectures as follows:

1 Knowledge: objective and subjective
2 Evolution, language and the third world
3 The myth of the framework
4 The interaction of the three worlds
5 Rationality
6 Freedom

But I have no intention of keeping strictly to this plan, and I regard it as a great advantage to have a connected course of six lectures. For this means that I do not need to worry about time: I can stop when the clock shows 3.50, saying that we shall continue next week. This is an advantage I do not want to forgo by tying each lecture to a definite topic. I may also change my mind while going along, especially if you, ladies and gentlemen, are willing to raise questions.

   This brings me to a technical point. I like to be interrupted, and to have questions put to me. And I ask you especially to interrupt my lecture whenever I say anything which is not quite clear. In fact, I prefer discussion to lecturing, and I shall regard myself free to change my plans for these lectures if any topic is raised in the

1

discussion here, or perhaps in the seminar, which seems to me to justify a change.

In addition to interruptions, there will be another possibility for you to raise questions. I shall stop at 3.50 for those who want to leave or who have to leave. But anybody who has time and who would like to stay on for discussion is invited to stay on and to ask questions.

I should like to tell you, especially since I see Professor Paul Kuntz in the audience, that you should not be afraid of me – in spite of what Professor Kuntz has written in the paper. I think I am misinterpreted by him: I am very meek and mild, and I have never in my life called anybody a blockhead – least of all a student. I might call a colleague a blockhead, but I can't remember having done so.

Another point which I wish to make before starting is this. I regard it as my first duty to my audience always to do my best to be easily understandable. I regard it as my second duty to let you always see which way I am going. This will enable you to consider my arguments critically, and especially to check whether I am misleading you.

I try to achieve this by presenting you with my problems, and usually even with my tentative solutions; and only afterwards shall I proceed to develop my arguments. In this way you can see in advance which way I am going, and can all the time look at my arguments *critically*.

It means that my course of lectures will have a kind of spiral structure.

Begin like this:

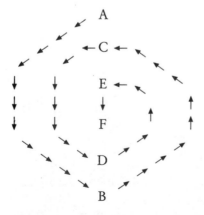

On the way from A to B, I give a broad outline of the problem in hand. This is then narrowed in stages, until we arrive at the tentative formulation F.

1. KNOWLEDGE: OBJECTIVE AND SUBJECTIVE

Now I will begin by explaining to you the two main sets of problems I intend to discuss. They are:

(A) the problem of two kinds of knowledge and their relationship:
    1 knowledge in the objective sense,
    2 knowledge in the subjective sense; and
(B) the body–mind problem or, as it is also called, the mind–body problem.

I will explain the first of these problems with the help of some examples.

1 We may say:
    '*It is well known that* water consists of hydrogen and oxygen'; or
    '*It is well known that* we can explain atomic and nuclear structures in terms of so-called elementary particles, but *it is not known* whether elementary particles have a structure in their turn: this is still an open problem.'

These examples explain what I mean by 'knowledge in the objective sense'.

2 The following examples may explain knowledge in the subjective sense:

    '*He knew* he was exceeding the speed limit.'
    '*He knew* that water is composed of hydrogen and oxygen.'

The following examples may also be treated under the heading of subjective knowledge, even though they are somewhat different:

    '*He thought* that elementary particles have an internal structure.'
    '*He observed* that the moon was full.'
    '*He observed* a yellow disk.'
    '*He saw* a yellow flash.'
    '*He hit* his shins.'
    '*He felt* a chill.'

I hope I have made the distinction between the two kinds of knowledge – objective knowledge and subjective knowledge – reasonably clear. It is interesting to note that most philosophers, though not all, discuss only knowledge in the subjective sense or (as I will say for brevity's sake) subjective knowledge. There exist many philosophical books devoted to the theory of knowledge, a theory which is also called 'epistemology', which never mention that there is such a thing as objective knowledge. And if they ever discuss objective knowledge, then most of them assume that objective knowledge can be fully explained in terms of subjective knowledge. In other words, it is assumed that objective knowledge consists of many elements of subjective knowledge somehow linked together.

I may tell you from the very start that for at least thirty-five years I have taken precisely the opposite view – without, however, making much impact. So here is a point where you will do well to look critically at what I am going to say.

My position is this: I am mainly interested in objective knowledge and its growth, and I contend that we cannot understand the first thing about subjective knowledge except by studying the growth of objective knowledge and the give and take between the two kinds of knowledge (where subjective knowledge is more taking than giving).

When I have finished my general introduction, the remainder of today's lecture will largely be devoted to this problem.

Why is this problem of knowledge important? Because it raises certain issues which I will here call 'big issues'. It bears on the big issue of rationality, on such big issues as the growth of scientific knowledge and its role in our civilization, on the big issues of the moral responsibility of the scientist and our indebtedness to civilization, and on the big issues of the function of a University and tradition *vs.* criticism. However, the problem of knowledge has a definite advantage over these big issues: it can be discussed in a critical and rational manner, while direct approach to any of the big issues is in danger of degenerating into preaching and of producing that hot air to which I am allergic, as I have said before.

The problem of knowledge will be one of my two main problems in this course. The other, you will recall, is:

(B) The body–mind problem or, as it is also called, the mind–body problem.

I will now explain this a little. We live in a world of physical bodies, and we ourselves have physical bodies. When I speak to you, however, I am addressing myself not to your bodies but to your minds. So in addition to the *first world*, the world of physical bodies and their physical and physiological states, which I will call 'world 1', there seems to exist a *second world*, the world of mental states, which I will call 'world 2'. And so a question arises concerning the

4

relationship between these two worlds, the world 1 of physical states or processes and the world 2 of mental states or processes. This question is the body–mind problem.

When I am talking to you I am, in the first instance, making some noises, which are physical events – physical events you can detect with the help of your ears, which are detectors of pressure waves. But you do not only detect these waves, you *decode* them: you hear meaningful sounds. These physical waves carry a meaning to you (or so I hope): they are significant – they may (and I hope they will) make you think.

According to the famous French philosopher René Descartes, also called 'Cartesius', my mind is now acting on my body, which produces physical sounds. These, in turn, are acting on your body, that is, on your ears; and then, your body is acting on your mind, making you think. Descartes and the Cartesians called this the 'interaction' between body and mind. And we may replace this by speaking about an *interaction* between *physical* and *mental* states.

I think that it is just common sense to accept, at least tentatively, that there exists indeed this interaction between physical states (or processes) and mental states (or processes), or between the worlds 1 and 2. And since things which interact may be said to be real, we may accept the reality of these two worlds. Thus I can describe myself as a Cartesian *dualist*. In fact I am doing a little better than even Descartes: I am a *pluralist*, for I also accept the reality of a *third world*, which I will call 'world 3'. I will very briefly explain this at once since it is my policy to put before you, from the very beginning, not only my problems but also my tentative solutions to these problems – and the theory of the reality of world 3 is the most important ingredient within my tentative solutions.

By 'world 3' I mean, roughly, the world of the *products* of our human minds. These products are sometimes physical things such as the sculptures, paintings, drawings, and buildings of Michelangelo. These *are* physical things, but they are a very peculiar kind of physical things: in my terminology they belong to both the worlds 1 *and* 3. Some other products of our minds are not precisely physical things. Take a play by Shakespeare. You may say that the written or printed book is a physical thing like, say, a drawing. But the performed play is clearly not a physical thing, though perhaps it may be said to be a highly complex sequence of physical events. But now please remember that no single performance of *Hamlet* can be said to be identical with Shakespeare's play *Hamlet* itself. Nor is

Shakespeare's play the class or set of all of its performances. The play may be said to be *represented* or *reproduced* by these performances, in a way similar to that in which a building or a sculpture may be said to be represented by one or several photographs, or in which a painting or a drawing may be said to be reproduced by prints of varying quality. But the original painting itself is different from its reproduction. And in a somewhat similar way, Shakespeare's *Hamlet* is, in itself, different from its various reproductions or performances. But while an original painting is, as we've said, a peculiar physical thing, Shakespeare's *Hamlet* clearly is not. Although its *reproductions* may be said to belong both to the world 1 of physical things and to the world 3 of products of the mind, the play, *Hamlet* itself, belongs *only* to the third world.

It is similar with a symphony. The written score of Mozart's Symphony in G Minor is not Mozart's symphony, although it represents Mozart's symphony in a coded form. And the various performances of Mozart's Symphony in G Minor are also not Mozart's symphony: they stand to the symphony in the relation of reproductions. These performances simultaneously belong to both world 1 and world 3. But the symphony itself belongs only to the third world – that third world which comprises architecture, art, literature, music and – perhaps *most* important – science and scholarship.

The idea of world 3 is, I realize, an unusual and a very difficult idea. So please don't think that you are supposed to grasp it fully at this first mention of it. Still, I think it best to put all my cards on the table at once, so that they are open for your inspection, and so that you can know which way I am going.

Incidentally, this reminds me of an anecdote. Many years ago, when I lived in New Zealand, I had a friend, old Dr Farr, an emeritus professor of physics, a famous student of geomagnetism, and known for his ready wit. When he was almost 80 years old he was still interested in the students of his old physics department and often talked to them in the street. One day a student was clearly embarrassed and, when asked 'What's wrong with you?', stammered: 'Excuse me, Dr Farr, but your hat is on the wrong way round!' Like a shot came back the reply: 'How do you know which way I am going?'

Now I do want you to know which way I am going, so that you can find out more easily what is wrong with me. Therefore I will now give you what, in a way, may be described as the main thesis of my course. It is this:

We cannot understand world 2, that is, the world inhabited by our own mental states, without understanding that its main function is to *produce* world 3 objects, and to be *acted upon* by world 3 objects. For world 2 interacts not only with world 1, as Descartes thought, but also with world 3; and world 3 objects can act upon world 1 only through world 2, which functions as an intermediary.

We can put this by way of a simple diagram:

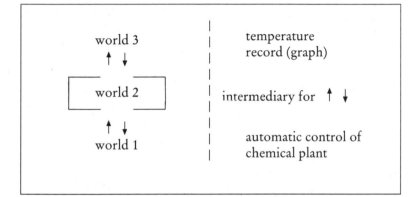

World 3 consists, among many other things, of records, and may consist of temperature records. In the case of temperature records, it may look as if here world 1, through a graph and an automatic recording instrument, acts directly upon something in world 3. But this is not so. It is we who arrange and are the intermediaries and make this temperature record and regulate the whole thing so that it really becomes a temperature recording, a graph, which belongs to both world 1 and world 3. It is only through our intermediary action that world 1 can act upon world 3.

A similar example in reverse would be the automatic control system of a chemical plant. Here again, world 3 – that is to say, certain objective plans and objective aims which exist in world 3 – somehow regulates what happens in the world 1 chemical plant through automatic machines. But these automatic machines must be installed by us, and it is only through us that the actual aims will have an effect upon world 1.

If my thesis is correct then we cannot expect to get anywhere near a solution of the body–mind problem unless we take world 3 into account. For the body–mind problem was the problem of the relationship between worlds 1 and 2. And if it is an important element in this relationship that world 2 functions as an intermediary between worlds 1 and 3, then the body–mind problem must remain incomplete, as it were, until we extend it to cover the interrelationships between all three worlds.

You may now understand why I said that I am not only a dualist but a pluralist. In this I am decidedly unfashionable. The prevailing fashion in philosophy is decidedly monistic, and it has been so for a long time. There have been quite different kinds of monism. Until not very long ago a school was fashionable which tried to interpret physical things as bundles of phenomena, or as observation possibilities, or as *constructs* of observations, or of sense data. That is to say, it was fashionable to try to reduce the first world to the second. This form of monism was called by various names, by 'phenomenalism' for example. At the present time another form of monism is more fashionable. It is called 'physicalism', or sometimes 'behaviourism', or 'materialism'. And it says that to accept what I call 'world 2' is to introduce unnecessary complications, since it is simpler and more convenient to say that only physical things and physical states exist. It is admitted that if I am talking to you I am making physical noises, and that my physiology has to be in an appropriate state for my doing so. It is also admitted that your self, or rather your physiology, may be incited to make some appropriate response to my noises. But it is held to be quite unnecessary to assume that we, you or I, are doing anything like paying attention or thinking.

Three of the outstanding physicalists are my friends Rudolph Carnap, Herbert Feigl, and Willard Van Orman Quine. The question is very concisely discussed by Quine, who acknowledges his indebtedness to Carnap and Feigl. Speaking about human behaviour, Quine questions whether anything can be gained by positing mental states behind behaviour. And Quine puts the matter in a nutshell by saying (I am quoting), 'The bodily states exist anyway; why add the others?' This is in his *Word and Object*, on page 264. It is interesting that very similar questions were asked by philosophers like Berkeley and Mach, who said: 'Sensations exist anyway; why add material things?'

I admit that the denial of mental states simplifies matters. For example, the difficult body–mind problem simply disappears, which no doubt is very convenient: it saves us the trouble of solving it. But I do not think that Quine is consistent when he asks 'Why add the others?' To whom does he address this question? To our bodies? Or to our physical states? Or to our behaviour? Quine *argues*. And arguments, I hold, belong to world 3. Arguments may be *understood*, or grasped. And understanding or grasping is a world 2 affair: our bodies can grasp a stone or a stick, but they cannot grasp or understand an argument.

Also, I am sure that it is Quine's *intention* (again a world 2 term) to *convince* us by his arguments, or at least to give us something to *think* about (two more world 2 terms).

Clearly he would not be *satisfied* (also a world 2 term) if he would only evoke a certain kind of behaviour in us – let us call it agreeing behaviour – such as the noises 'Exactly!' or 'That is so!' or 'Well done!'

This ends my criticism of Quine.

Pluralism, at any rate, is out of fashion, just as objective knowledge is out of fashion and, I am afraid, *most* of the things I shall be saying in these lectures are out of fashion. (I hope they will remain out of fashion.)

In connection with our first problem, the problem of knowledge, I asked earlier why the problem was important. And I replied with a list of what I called 'big issues' (such as rationality). Similarly, there are also a number of big issues behind the body–mind problem and its extended form, the problem of the three worlds. For example, there are the big issues of human freedom, and of the control we have over our lives; the big issue of human creativity; and perhaps the biggest issue of all: our relations to our actions, and especially to our work, and how we ourselves can grow through our work. But please, remember what I said about the dangers of the big issues.

Ladies and Gentlemen, we have gone very quickly over the two main problems of a course planned for six lectures – indeed, it was almost a race, and I think we may all feel a bit out of breath.

So let us stop for a moment and recapitulate. But please remember where we are. We are still only approaching the end of an introduction to our course, an introduction in the form of a survey. I have just sketched our two main problems (A) and (B), the problem of knowledge (A), and the body–mind problem (B). And I have indicated to you which way I shall be going. In connection with the problem of knowledge (A), I shall be stressing the importance of objective knowledge. And in connection with the body–mind problem (B), I shall be stressing the importance of world 3. This, in brief, is my programme discussed so far.

But I have not so far said anything about the connection between the two problems, (A) and (B). This connection is, of course, very important. It may be stated as follows:

> Objective knowledge belongs itself to world 3. It constitutes the biologically most important part of world 3, and that part which has the most important repercussions upon world 1.

Objective knowledge consists of guesses, hypotheses, or theories – usually published in the form of books, journals, or lectures. It also consists of unsolved *problems*, and of *arguments* for and against the various competing theories. It is therefore clear that objective knowledge forms part of the world 3 of mental products. Thus the growth of objective knowledge will be part of the growth of world 3. And this gives us a clue for understanding *how* the third world could ever evolve. From the point of view of biological evolution, it originally evolved because of its tremendous survival value. If you remember the significance of world 3 for the body–mind problem, then you will see that here is also a clue for a biological under-standing of the evolution of the human mind: the human mind evolved together with world 3, and with objective knowledge.

Thus my approach to the solution of our problems and especially our approach to world 3 will be biologically oriented: it will make use of *evolutionary* ideas. This may perhaps surprise you if you consider how very abstract and abstruse and, indeed, 'philosophical' is this idea of a world 3.

With this, I conclude for the time being my outline of the main problems of our course of lectures.

Having completed my introduction to the course I now proceed to the special topic of today's lecture – 'Knowledge: objective and subjec-tive'. As usual, I will start by stating my problem and my solution.

My problem is: how does our knowledge grow?

My solution is a somewhat oversimplified tetradic schema of the method of trial and of error elimination:

$$P_1 \rightarrow TT \rightarrow EE \rightarrow P_2$$

Here 'P_1' means the problem from which we start. It may be a practical or a theoretical problem.

'TT' is a tentative theory which we offer in order to solve that problem.

'EE' means a process of error elimination, by way of critical tests, or of critical discussion.

'P_2' means the problems with which we end – the problems which emerge from the discussions and tests.

The whole schema indicates that we start from a problem, either a practical problem or a theoretical problem. We try to solve it by producing a tentative theory as our tentative solution: this is our trial. We then put our theory to the test, trying to fail it: this is the critical method of error elimination. As a result of all this a new problem, P_2, arises (or perhaps several new problems). The progress made, or the growth of our knowledge achieved, can usually be estimated by the distance between P_1 and P_2, and we will then know if we have made any progress. In brief, our schema says that *knowledge starts from problems and ends with problems* (so far as it ever ends).

P_1 is often a practical problem, but it may be a theoretical problem. The same holds for P_2.

This schema is applicable to knowledge in the objective and in the subjective sense. We shall see that its range of application is even much wider than this.

Let me take an example from the growth of objective knowledge which starts from a practical problem and ends with a practical problem. Henry Ford's original problem was: how can we provide transport for the vast spaces of the United States? This was his P_1. He proposed the theory: by building a cheap motor car. This led through various trials and errors to a new problem: how can we provide the roads and parking places needed for our cars? The original problem P_1 was the problem of transport. The new problem P_2 is the traffic problem – a problem of frustration.

More often than not the problems are theoretical. A typical theoretical problem is: why are there these strange stars that are erring about the sky instead of sticking to their place and rotating with the sky, as the vast majority of the stars do? The Greek name for erring stars is 'planets', and this problem led, through many stages, to Ptolemy, and to Copernicus and Kepler, and to Newton's theory, which first unified celestial and terrestrial physics. But this was not the end: unsolved problems remained, as Newton himself pointed out in his *Optics*, and they led, after another 200 years, to Einstein. And Einstein pointed out problems unsolved by his theory. And so the story goes on and on.

Our tetradic schema may be elaborated in various ways. For

11

example, we may replace it by the following schema:

$$P_1 \to \quad \begin{matrix} \nearrow \\ \\ \searrow \end{matrix} \quad \begin{matrix} TT_a \to EE_a \to P_{2a} \\ TT_b \to EE_b \to P_{2b} \to \\ TT_n \to EE_n \to P_{2n} \end{matrix} \quad \begin{matrix} \searrow \\ \\ \nearrow \end{matrix} \quad CED$$

Here we have several competing theories, each giving rise to new tests – to attempts to fail the theories – and to new problems. *CED* stands here for 'critical evaluative discussion': in this one attempts to decide which of the competing theories are good enough to survive, and which should be eliminated altogether.

The schema shows that we can look at the growth of knowledge as if it were a struggle for survival between the competing theories. Only the fittest theories survive, though they too may be killed at any moment.

If we compare this with Darwinian natural selection, then we can see at once the tremendous biological advantage of the evolution of a world 3 of objective knowledge.

An individual or species will be eliminated if it comes forth with a mistaken solution to a problem. This holds for mistaken mutations (so-called lethal mutations), and it holds for mistaken knowledge in the subjective sense: a so-called 'error of judgement' may easily lead to the elimination of the person who made that error of judgement (if he is a driver he may take others with him). A story which I often tell is the story of an Indian community that thought that life was holy, even the life of tigers. As a consequence the community disappeared and with it the theory that the life of tigers is holy. But objective knowledge is different: *we can let our objective theories die in our stead.* Actually, we do our best to kill them, by testing them severely, before we use them. In this way, a thousand theories may be killed any day without anybody being the worse off.

These considerations point towards a wider application of our original tetradic schema:

$$P_1 \to TT \to EE \to P_2$$

We may apply it to biological evolution, not only to knowledge – to the evolution, for example, of a certain species of moth. The problem will be practical for the moth: it may be created by a change in the environment, perhaps through industrialization. *TT*, then, will not be a tentative theory, but a mutation: say a change in colour. *EE* is error elimination through natural selection: only the fittest mutations survive, until the next problem arises.

We thus can look at human theory formation – that is, at objective knowledge – as something like a *mutation outside our skin* or, as it is called, an 'exosomatic mutation'. Theories are in this respect (but not in all respects) like instruments, for instruments are like exosomatic organs. Instead of growing better eyes, we grow binoculars and spectacles. Instead of growing better ears, we grow microphones, loudspeakers, and hearing aids. And instead of growing faster legs, we grow motor cars.

So much about objective knowledge. As for subjective knowledge, much of it is simply taken over from objective knowledge. We learn a great deal from books, and in universities. But the opposite does not hold: although objective knowledge is man-made, it is rarely made by taking over subjective knowledge. It happens very rarely that a man first forms a conviction on the basis of personal experience, publishes it, and gets it objectively accepted as one of the things of which we say 'It is known that …'. As a rule, objective knowledge is the result of competing theories offered tentatively to some objectively known problem. And it is accepted into the objective domain, or the public domain, only after prolonged critical discussion based on tests.

If this is so, then it follows that subjective knowledge rarely becomes objective and, further, that no theory of subjective knowledge will be able to account for objective knowledge. This must be developed: a piece of subjective knowledge (world 2) becomes objective (world 3 criticizable) by formulation in some language.

Our tetradic schema, on the other hand, can account for both.

I said before that an important part of subjective knowledge is objective knowledge taken over by some subject. But it is easy to show that the largest part of subjective knowledge consists in inborn potentialities: in dispositions, or in modifications of inborn dispositions.

First of all, most things a man knows consist in dispositions. If a man knows how to ride a bicycle or how to play the violin, then this knowledge clearly consists of dispositions to do the right things in certain situations. If we say he knows differential and integral calculus, then again we mean he knows how to differentiate and integrate: he has acquired dispositional knowledge. The same holds for the knowledge of languages.

Similarly, knowledge consisting in *information*, knowledge *that* things are such and such – for example, that the present President of the United States is Richard Nixon, and that the present Sovereign of England is Elizabeth II – consists essentially in the *disposition* to remember what we have read or heard about certain things, and in the disposition to *expect* certain things and not to expect other things. If any of you read in tomorrow's newspaper that President Humphrey has, after a visit to Europe, returned to the White House, you would be shocked and bewildered, because this report runs counter to your expectations – that is, to some kind of dispositions.

We thus can describe all kinds of subjective knowledge as consisting of dispositions to react in certain ways to certain situations. Now in men and in animals, most dispositions to react in certain ways to certain situations are inborn. And if not inborn but acquired, they are acquired by the utilization or modification of inborn dispositions. For example, speaking English or French is an acquired disposition. But the basis – the disposition to learn some human language – is an inborn characteristic of the human species alone.

All inborn dispositions have been acquired by the species, for all we know, by natural selection, which is essentially a method of trial and error elimination – a method that is described in an over-simplified way by our tetradic schema.

I have given you some rough idea of a theory of knowledge. It is very far removed from what is still usually taught as the theory of knowledge.

Most philosophical theories of knowledge are still pre-Darwinian. They do not look upon knowledge as the result of natural selection. The following is a somewhat ironical presentation, but by no means an outdated one. Moreover, it is accepted by common sense and by many philosophers too.

I call it the 'bucket theory of the mind'. It may be represented by the following diagram.

It starts from the problem: how do I know? The answer is: I gain knowledge through my senses – through the eyes, the ears, the nose, and the tongue; through these it enters into my bucket. Of course, it also enters through the sense of touch, which is not presented in my schema.

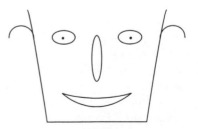

How do I acquire knowledge through the senses? The usual answer is: stimuli coming from the external world impinge on our senses and are transformed into sense-data or sensations or perceptions. After many stimuli are thus received, we discover similarities in our sense-material. Thus repetition becomes possible, and through repetition we arrive at generalizations or rules, and so we are led, by habit, to the expectation of regularities.

This, in brief, is the theory which was elaborated and refined by the great British philosophers Locke, Berkeley, and Hume. These philosophers lived before Darwin. I do not think that after Darwin anybody had any longer any right to think along lines such as these.

First of all, expectations do in fact precede similarities and repetition. The newborn child or the newborn calf expects to be fed. It knows how to suck, and it expects to be offered something to suck. In newborn cats this comes long before they open their eyes.

Second, logical reasons can be given why this must be so: without inborn dispositions – dispositions to learn – we never could learn anything.

Third, there are children born blind and deaf. They may not only learn to speak in terms of a touch language, but they may become great writers and fully capable human beings. Admittedly, they need *some* sense such as the sense of touch. But the main thing is that their intellect, their imagination, does not need either the eyes or the ears to operate. The basis of their development is their maturing innate knowledge, their maturing disposition to learn a human language. And once they have learned a language, they can, as it were, plug into the third world. And with this, all the worlds open up to them.

The decisive point is the innate disposition to learn a language: this provides us with the key to the third world.

DISCUSSION

Questioner 1: The following question is really a short one. I think I could say it is well known that you are not an 'instrumentalist' as that term is being used, and yet you yourself did indicate that, in a sense, your explanation of knowledge in terms of the analogy of evolution, of competing theories, did give rise to a kind of feeling that theories were instruments for survival.

Popper: My view is that theories are, amongst other things, instruments, but they are not *only* instruments. The main difference is that I cannot say of an instrument that it is true or false. I can say only that it is a good instrument or a bad instrument, and that it is good or bad only for a certain purpose. For example, a bicycle is a very good instrument for certain purposes, even though for other purposes it has been superseded by the motor car. But this does not mean that it is not good for other purposes. There is competition, of course, between instruments – no doubt. But there is also the fact that superseded instruments may still be very good if we have nothing better at hand. We may be very glad to have a screwdriver even though it is not one of the most modern ones, and so on.

With theories the situation is different. Theories are instruments, but they are also something else. A theory can be true or false. We may be unable to decide whether it is true or false, but we are very often able to judge theories from the point of view of whether one theory is a better approximation to the truth than another theory.

So, for example, physicists and astronomers generally agree that Newtonian theory is a better approximation to the truth than, let us say, Ptolemy's theories or Kepler's theory or Galileo's theory. So there arises a new problem now – namely the problem of the relation of theories to truth – and it is actually this problem, the problem of truth and the possibility of arguing about the truth of a theory, which opens up a whole characteristically human part of world 3. The most important part of world 3 consists of theories, problems, and arguments. This part of world 3 is dominated by such ideas as truth, or approximation to truth – the validity and invalidity of arguments. So I would usually say that I am not an instrumentalist, if instrumentalism is the view that theories are nothing but instruments. But everybody agrees that theories are instruments. The question is whether they are anything but instruments. That is the issue of so-called 'instrumentalism'.

Questioner 1: That is true, but many of our world 3 theories do not do too well as instruments for survival.... [laughter]

Popper: Certainly! There is nothing to be laughed about – it is certainly so. As a matter of fact, I shall later discuss how all sorts of things which cannot be explained merely from the survival point of view appear, as it were, in world 3 – how these things develop in world 3. I will discuss especially how we may create new aims, or new purposes. And the creation of such aims and purposes may have no survival value at all as such. But once they are created, all sorts of things become important in world 3 because they are related to these new aims and purposes.

In other words, I am not an instrumentalist because instrumentalism says that theories are nothing but instruments. That is the point. I do not think anybody can seriously deny that theories are instruments. But they are something else also. Let us say that theories *may* be instruments. Not every theory needs to be an instrument.

Questioner 2: Sir Karl, I think that many systematic American philosophers who deal with 'what there is' are convinced that your pluralism is the correct answer to these monistic attempts. And in the light of that, I would like to ask whether you can prove that there are *only* three worlds. You have said that there are at least three worlds, but you have not said that there are three and only three worlds. And I wish to ask specifically against the background of American philosophy dealing with 'modes of being' or 'realms of being', as had Santayana and as has Weiss, because each of them has a sort of 'fourth realm' in which there are norms such as truth, in which there are ideals, and I was struck by the fact that the word 'right' appeared when you talked about subjective knowledge – the endeavour of a person who knows how to speak or how to play, to play right. Now since truth probably enters into your definition of objective knowledge, and for a proposition to be true is an ideal – it is better for a proposition to be true rather than false – isn't there room for a fourth realm: some fourth realm of norms? And then you have the problem as to whether *that* is man-made, as is your third realm, or as to whether we have discovered in the nature of things a certain normative character that we attempt both through subjective and objective knowledge to fulfil.

Popper: I would say that really the name 'world 3' is just a way of putting things, and the thing is not to be taken too seriously. We can speak about it as a world, we can speak about it as just a certain region. I call it 'real' because it interacts with us and with physical things.

Interaction seems to me to be a kind of not perhaps necessary, but *sufficient* criterion of reality. When you see the bulldozers flattening a piece of land, then you actually see the action of world 3 upon world 1 very clearly, because there are plans behind the bulldozer. When you look at it, it may look quite planless. But you know that each push of the bulldozer is done with the intention of realizing

17

some blueprint of an airfield, or whatever it may be. These plans are obviously third world in my sense since they are man-made, and they operate on the first world of physical things. If you build a house, and so on – all that is the same thing.

Now, whether or not you distinguish further regions or worlds is really only a matter of convenience. Aims, as I have said before, operate on world 1 through us, and belong to world 3. But of course you can take them out and put them in a world of their own. I would not mind in the least, and I would not argue about such things. This is really a matter of convenience. For some purposes it may be very convenient to have it, and for other purposes it may be quite sufficient to leave them in. It depends on the problems we are discussing, and we do not need to cross the bridges before we come to them. This is connected with what you said about definition. I am afraid I am probably – I do not know – the only philosopher who abhors definitions. I believe that definition is a logical problem of its own, and that an incredible amount of superstition is attached to it. People think that a term has no meaning unless you have defined it. But it can be easily shown, with a few little logical considerations, that this is obviously nonsense. I do not say that definitions may not have a role to play in connection with certain problems, but I do say it is for most problems quite irrelevant whether a term can be defined or cannot be defined, or how it is defined. All that is necessary is that we make ourselves understood. And definition is certainly not a means of making oneself understood.

Aristotle has several definitions for 'man'. One is 'man is a featherless biped', and I am sure a 'featherless biped' is not as understandable as 'man'. The other is that 'man is a rational animal'. I am also pretty sure that 'rational', for example, is a much more difficult term than 'man'.

So, by and large, definitions do not contribute to making oneself understood or making things clear. I mention this because it always comes up in practically every lecture I give, that I have to dissociate myself from the problem of definition. Now, you suggested that I should define truth, and world 3, and knowledge, and so on. I do not define these things. Truth is something very important. It so happens that another friend of mine, Alfred Tarski, has given a definition of truth. But here the problem was that the concept of truth was under attack by philosophers and by logicians. Certain people said that truth was a meaningless idea. In such a situation of course it is rescuing the honour of the suspect idea if one can show that it is definable in non-suspect terms. And this is really the philosophical significance of Tarski's definition of truth. He, as it were, rescued truth from infamy.

Now, if in such a context somebody defines something, it is very good. But we do not need to define truth, although we can explain what we mean by 'truth'. To explain what we mean in a very informal sort of conversation depends not only on the speaker but also on his listeners: he has to ask them, 'Are you now satisfied, or are you not satisfied?' It is very different from a definition which is just thrown at you – and you just have to accept it and stagger under the impact. So I think it necessary to say this.

In this sense I am not dreaming of defining a concept like world 1, world 2, or world 3. I explain these things by examples and if you do not feel satisfied I will add new examples, and I will ask you where the difficulty is. But I shall certainly not always give a definition.

Now world 3 of course consists of many different regions. The arts are in some way different from the sciences, but in some way they are all similar. They are all somehow or other products of man, and they are all in some sense or other *autonomous*. This I will discuss another time – what I call the 'autonomy' of world 3 – but perhaps now, I do not see why I should not mention it at once.

We may say that with the invention of a sufficiently rich language, the Babylonians were the first, so far as we know, who designed a number system in which one can go on and on and on. And we have a similar number system: it is the endless series of natural numbers – 1, 2, 3, 4, and so on. And there is a method in this system by which we know how to go on and on and on beyond any given point. So the number system may be said to be man-made. Some people have said it is made by God. The mathematician Kronecker has said that the natural numbers are made by God, and that everything else in mathematics is the work of man. Now take such a thing as odd and even numbers. These are not made by us. They *emerge* from the series of natural numbers. You cannot make a series of natural numbers without creating odd numbers and even numbers. You may not notice it – you may not know that you have created odd numbers and even numbers, but you do create them – and this is what I would describe as the autonomy of the system. And every world 3 object has a kind of autonomy of this kind – that is to say, something which we have not made but which is an unintended consequence of what we *have* made. Amongst the unintended consequences are, of course, not only the odd and even numbers but, very interesting, the prime numbers. You probably know what prime numbers are – numbers which are not divisible except by themselves and by the number 1. So 2, 3, 5, 7, 11, and 13 and so on are prime numbers. Now, prime numbers not only have not been made by us but are already quite beyond our control in a certain sense. We do not even know much about their distribution. We cannot give a general formula for a prime number. We cannot, except by working it out with the help of trial-and-error methods, say of a very big number whether it is prime or not. This has to be done by just trying to divide it first by 2 – that is easy enough – then by 3 – that also is fairly easy. But when it comes to bigger numbers – to 23 for example – it may no longer be so easy, and it may in fact be very difficult to see whether or not a number is divisible by 23. Only after we have tried very many prime numbers – as a matter of fact something like a fifth or so, a seventh of that number – only after we have tried them can we know whether or not this number is prime.

Now this shows that there is something here to be discovered. Although the numbers are made by us, there are certain things about them which are not made by us, but which can be discovered by us. And this is what I call the 'autonomy' of world 3. It is to be distinguished from what I call the 'reality' of world 3, which is connected with the fact that we may interact with it. But the third world is both autonomous and real. This is one of my main points.

But you are quite right – there have been quite a number of American philosophers who were pluralists, and I am especially near in my position to Peirce. But I have also to say that I discovered Peirce very late in my life and therefore I have no very great familiarity with him, unfortunately.

Questioner 3: I want you to dispel two misunderstandings I might have before we go any further. Since I am in the visual arts, and since I notice that you are fond of diagrams, I wanted to be sure that I was not mistaken in assuming that your diagram of the first, second, and third worlds was not, on the one hand, hierarchical – or that you were placing the second world in a middle position which made the other two worlds as it were ancillary to the second.

Popper: No, the second world is indeed in an intermediary position, though the other worlds are by no means ancillary to it. But in a way, putting it from below – first, second, third – I mean an evolutionary hierarchy. For all we know world 1 existed before the second world existed, and at least the rudiments of world 2 existed before the third world existed. But I think the full development of world 2 is only in interaction with world 3, and this will be one of the things I want to discuss in some detail. Also, if there is an ancillary position I would say world 2 is in an ancillary position to the third rather than the other way round. Even in an ancillary position to the first, especially if we take certain kinds of animal life and assume that there exists a second world. I think these are all questions which I intend to discuss.

Questioner 4: There are two things I would like to have clarified. Did the play *Hamlet* exist in the mind of Shakespeare? And if so, did it exist in both world 3 and world 2 simultaneously?

Popper: I wonder whether *Hamlet* as a whole existed in the mind of Shakespeare. It is very difficult to answer. I mean, what is *Hamlet* as a whole? It is certainly the work of the mind of Shakespeare. Each part certainly existed in a certain stage. But whether Shakespeare at any moment really had the whole play in his mind is more than doubtful. It is said of Mozart – there exists a letter of Mozart in which Mozart says that – I have forgotten whether it is an overture or a symphony – that this existed in his mind as a whole. Fortunately this letter has been shown to be a forgery. It is still quoted in many books about aesthetics, but it is not a genuine letter. I don't think that Shakespeare could have *Hamlet* without really writing it. It isn't so that we have first the thing perfect in our mind and then write it down. It is always a process of creating which is like the process of a painter. A painter has a canvas and he may put here a colour spot on and step back and see the effect of the colour spot, and he may perhaps eliminate it. Or he may see that the colour spot alters his whole aim. The colour spot may suggest to him a change in plan. It may be that new ideas arise in the painter's mind. There is a give and take – and this will also be one of my main points, namely, the constant give and take between the second and the third worlds. Even while we create something there is a constant give and take. Most writers do constantly change what they have written, or again and again change it. Not all: Bertrand Russell has shown me some manuscripts of his in which there is about one correction per page, and a very small correction. But there are few writers who write like this and as a rule – I mean it is at least so with me – I begin to write when I think I have the thing completely in my mind. But when it is there after many, many corrections, it is something very different from what I had in mind, and I have learnt a lot by trying to write it down, to correct it and improve it. So I do think it can hardly be said – we cannot be sure: it is possible, but we can hardly be sure – that *Hamlet* was ever in the mind of Shakespeare before it was created, before it was actually written down. Very likely it was a process in which the actual progress of the play suggested new ideas to Shakespeare which he did not have before. There was most likely give and take between this thing and the author. I think really that all we can say is that there is such an entity as *Hamlet*, and that it is neither the book nor the handwriting, because, after all, the book is only a book for a play, and the handwriting is the handwriting for a play. Nor is it any particular performance. You see, just as the reproduction of an original is different from the original of a painting and can be very bad, the reproduction of a play can be very bad. Somehow or other there exists this idea of *Hamlet* as a play in the third world and it is differently interpreted by different minds.

Questioner 4: The second area which I was a little unsure of – I guess there are two questions here and both of them are very closely related. One of them is based on the world 3 concept. You sometimes refer to this as a product of the mind, and sometimes as a product of the *human* mind. Are you limiting it to the human mind? And second, would instinctual behaviour or unlearned behaviour be part of world 3?

Popper: This is an interesting and very difficult question. It is perhaps better to say 'no', but certainly we can construct a concept of world 3 where the answer would be 'yes'. It depends. Or one may even say – it is also a question I intend to discuss – one may extend the world 3 idea to the animal world. A spider makes a spider's web. Now that web is a product of the spider. Honey is the product of bees. You can include all animal products, except waste products – you can include all animal products in world 3 if you like. This would be quite good. It would be an extension of the concept, but then the human world 3 would still be a very important district in this third world. As a matter of fact, I will say so now, that I had this world 3 for many years and did not in a sense dare to publish anything about it because it was too absurd and too abstruse – until I realized that one could give it an evolutionary explanation by linking it with animal products, and by showing that, after all, architecture is like nests built by birds or by bees, only somewhat more complicated. And also less instinctive. All that is important for the human case, extremely important. But also, the possibility of linking it to animals in general is very important to take away the shadiness of the concept, which it otherwise has, especially in such cases as *Hamlet*.

Questioner 5: I have just two questions. (1) I wonder what the status of the problem, or the problematic, is in your three worlds, as it were. I can see where *theory* is a creation of the human mind. But what about the problematic? What is the nature of the problematic?

Popper: The problem was originally the body–mind problem.

Questioner 5: No, I am talking about a problematic itself. Where would one put a problem?

Popper: One puts the problem in world 3.

Questioner 5: I have difficulties in seeing that problems should exist in world 3. I would think that a question about a problem would exist in world 3, but the problem itself is in world 1.

Popper: Let us say a theoretical problem is in world 3. A *practical* problem may not exist in world 3, but a theoretical problem is man-made, or originates like the prime number problems: it originates from world 3 and therefore belongs to world 3. Theoretical problems certainly belong to world 3.

Questioner 5: The other question would be: (2) Could computers add to world 3, add theories to world 3? I mean, they come up with new theories. Are they thinking things? Or do they add to the world?

Popper: No, they are themselves man-made things. I do think that computers are very important and very interesting, but they should not be overrated. Einstein, before the computer age, once said, 'My pencil is cleverer than I am.' And that is clear enough: he would not use the pencil unless the pencil were in some way cleverer than he himself. Now I would say a computer is nothing more than a glorified pencil. So let us not only debunk men, but let us also debunk computers for a change.

Shall we stop? Thank you.

2

THE AUTONOMY OF
WORLD 3

Ladies and Gentlemen:

Let me begin by briefly reminding you of the two main problems which I want to discuss in this course. The first I dubbed the 'problem of knowledge', a name by which I mean here, more specifically, the problem of the relation between knowledge in the objective sense and knowledge in the subjective sense. The second is the body–mind or mind–body problem, the problem of the relation between physical states and mental states, or between what I call 'world 1' states and 'world 2' states. This second problem I extended to cover what I propose to call 'world 3' – that is, the world of products of the human mind.

> *World 3*
> *World 2*
> *World 1*

This summary covers the first half of my last lecture. In the second half I briefly discussed the problem of knowledge. I distinguished objective knowledge – which consists of problems, theories, and arguments – from subjective knowledge – which consists of dispositions and, among these, dispositions to expect, or *expectations*. I further explained especially my tetradic schema of the growth of knowledge.

$$P_1 \rightarrow TT \rightarrow EE \rightarrow P_2$$

After this I began, briefly, with a criticism of the traditional theory of knowledge. It is a theory of *subjective* knowledge, and it is still very widely held. It may be schematically represented as the bucket theory of the mind, which in the history of philosophy is well known as the theory of the *tabula rasa*, or the 'empty blackboard', on which experience is to engrave its findings.

I sketched it by drawing the following diagram:

According to this theory, the four senses represented in the schema plus the sense of touch are the sources of all our knowl-edge. I gave you some reasons why I think that this theory is completely mistaken. Amongst others: that most of the disposi-tions which constitute our knowledge are inborn, or hereditary; that most of those which are not inborn are modifications of inborn dispositions; and that the remainder are taken over from objective knowledge, and are not subjective at all. So, actually, nothing remains of the 'bucket theory' – it is wrong on all counts. I criticized this theory briefly, and I originally intended to proceed today with this criticism, and also with my own theory of the growth of knowledge.

But on the basis of the discussion we had after the first lecture, I have changed my mind with respect to the further lectures, and especially with respect to today's lecture. For almost all the questions raised last time were about world 3. At any rate, I had foreseen that I might have to change my plans, and I am doing so now. I will now proceed to a discussion of world 3 – partly summing up the discussion we had after the lecture last week – and afterwards I will, if time permits and so far as time permits, begin a discussion of the biological and evolutionary background of world 3.

So let me now turn to world 3 itself.

As I mentioned in my first lecture last Thursday, what I call 'world 3' may be described, very roughly, as the world of the products of the human mind. To it belong the products of architecture, art, literature, music, scholarship and, most important of all, the problems, theories and critical discussions of the sciences.

Of course, the name 'world 3' is a metaphor: we could, if we wish to, distinguish more than three worlds. We could, for example, distinguish the world of objective knowledge as a separate world from that of the arts, and other distinctions would also be possible. But I do not wish to make any more fuss than is needed for our main purposes.

Now when I said that the name 'world 3' was a metaphor, I did not say everything about it. For it is a bit more than a metaphor. It is also a bit more than a world of products of the mind. I have indicated some of this in my first lecture and in the discussion, but I shall explain it more fully now.

Take as an example geometry. It is obviously man-made, and we even have some historical tradition of its origin in Egypt and in Babylon: it served first the instrumental purpose of measuring land, probably in order to help in assessing a land tax.

The idea of using whenever possible only straight lines and circles in geometry is also clearly a man-made tradition – and so is the idea of a right angle. But it is not a man-made fact that for every circle the following proposition or theorem holds: draw a diameter; choose any point on the circumference other than an end point of the diameter, and connect by straight lines the chosen point with the two end points; then these lines will form a right angle at the chosen point.

A geometrical proposition or theorem like the one just stated is typically not made by us. It arises as an *unintended consequence* of our invention of geometry, of compasses and of circles, and of the straight edge and the straight line. There are, of course, hundreds of such theorems, and also much deeper ones. But with any such theorem there also arise new problems, such as how can the theorem be proved? (Only when it has been proved do we call it a 'theorem' – before that we call it a 'conjecture'.) That is, how is it connected with other geometrical propositions? Our particular theorem follows indeed almost immediately from two propositions: the one that the sum of the angles in every triangle is equal to two right angles (which together form a straight line), a proposition which according to Aristotle exhibits the essence of the triangle; and the other that if in a triangle two sides are equal, then the two angles between these and the third side are also equal.

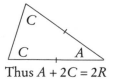
Thus $A + 2C = 2R$

From this proposition and from the one that the sum of the angles is equal to two right angles, and further from the definition of the circle which says that all its radii are equal, we get a proof which a dubious interpretation of a tradition ascribes to the founder of Greek philosophy, Thales:

$$A + B = 2R$$
$$A + 2C = 2R$$
$$/\therefore \quad B = 2C$$
$$/\therefore \quad C = B/2$$

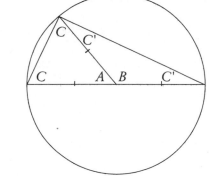

Similarly,

$$A + B = 2R$$
$$B + 2C' = 2R$$
$$/\therefore \quad A = 2C'$$
$$/\therefore \quad C' = A/2$$

$$/\therefore \quad C + C' = A/2 + B/2 = 1R$$

Thus the theorems, the problems, and, of course, the arguments which we call 'proofs' are all unintended consequences of our invention of geometry.

These unintended consequences can be discovered, just as we may discover a mountain or a river – which shows that they were there before our discovery.

If you have followed the proof, then you have been following, in your own subjective ways, a world 3 argument. You have, as it were, *plugged* into a world 3 product of the philosopher Thales. It is a case of *interaction* between two minds *through the world 3 product*.

World 3:	Proof	
World 2:	Thales	You
World 1:		

But the important thing is that, for your understanding of the argument, Thales and his mind have become quite unimportant. It is in fact very likely that the interpretation of the story which attributes an argument like this to Thales is mistaken. Or perhaps Thales produced a different proof. All of this is irrelevant for your understanding of the argument. This you do by plugging into world 3 – that is, by following the world 3 argument as such. The proof I have given you may be described as a *discursive* proof. There are a number of definite steps, and a calculation, and it all ends with a kind of surprise, and perhaps the feeling that a trick has been played on us.

But there is also a proof which is less discursive and which seems more *intuitive*. We start from observing that to every rectangle – that is, a figure with four right angles – can be circumscribed a circle. We have only to draw the diagonals to see this.

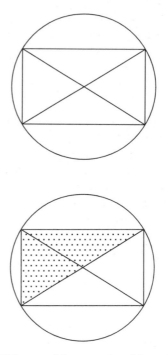

But any of the diagonals is obviously a diameter of the circumscribed circle, and half of the rectangle cut off by the diagonal is obviously a rectangular triangle of the kind we have discussed. All this is quite immediate. In order to get our proof, we have only to reverse the procedure, and to note that no other parallelogram except a rectangular one has equal diagonals.

This proof is more intuitive: the symmetries involved can be understood at a glance. Understanding it is, as it were, less dependent upon the argument. All one has to do is to complete the triangle into a parallelogram. The intuitive character of the proof is felt in this way: one can turn it more easily into subjective knowledge than the discursive proof. And yet it is a world 3 discovery, and it solves a world 3 problem, just as much as the first proof. Besides, it is in need of a supporting argument or proof which I have not really given: that no parallelogram can have a circle circumscribed to it unless the parallelogram has four right angles. However, even without going into this supporting argument, our intuitive argument is pretty convincing.

Now I have shown you these very simple arguments not because I wish to teach you geometry. Nothing is further from my mind, and this, in any event, would not be the right way to go about it. Rather, I want to discuss the role of world 3 – the role, that is, of objective problems, arguments, and theories. I want to discuss the importance of the fact that these problems, arguments, and theories can be *discovered* – that they can be *found*. And I want especially to discuss the fact that these problems, arguments, and theories can be *understood* by us and that this understanding or grasping is not like the understanding of another person and his intentions, but is, on the contrary, just this peculiar thing: the understanding of an objective problem, argument, or theory.

It will now be easy for you to distinguish two senses of thought, the objective and the subjective sense:

Thought in the *subjective* sense is a thinking process that can differ vastly from occasion to occasion and from person to person. In the case of our example, it may consist in realizing that the three lines are radii and thus equally long.

It happens *at a certain time*.

Thought in the *objective* sense is the content of some statement (or assertion or proposition), or the connectedness of an argument, or the difficulty which constitutes an unsolved problem. Though it may have been invented, or else found or discovered at a certain time, it can be plugged into or subjectively understood at *any* time after. As a world 3 inmate, it becomes what may be called 'timeless'. But it has a temporal history.

I have said earlier that new problems and new arguments arise as the unintended consequences of our invention of geometry.

Similarly, as I said last time in the discussion, we may invent a method of naming the natural numbers so that we can, in principle, always add one, and so go on to infinity. This is our invention, in this case belonging to the Babylonians. But from this invention there emerge unintended and unavoidable consequences which we neither invent, nor make, but discover. For example, that there are odd and even numbers; or that there are divisible numbers and prime numbers such as 2, 3, 5, 7, 11, 13, 17, 19, 23, 29, and 31. These prime numbers have given rise to many solved and many more yet unsolved problems. For example, the problem 'Does the sequence of prime numbers fizzle out or do they go on for ever?' has been solved by Euclid. Although they occur less and less often as we go along, they never fizzle out: there is no end to them. Euclid's proof is very simple and very beautiful, but I do not have enough time to state it here. There are lots of unsolved problems, for example: 'Do twin primes fizzle out?' (Twin primes are primes with exactly one even number between them, such as 3 & 5; 5 & 7; 11 & 13; 17 & 19; 29 & 31. They are called 'twin primes' because they are very close to each other, as close as two primes can possibly be to each other.) Now the question whether or not the twin primes fizzle out is one of the unsolved problems of number theory. We just do not know. We know that they go on for very long, but we do not know whether they go on for ever. In order to know that for certain we would have to prove it – that is to say, to derive it from the structure of the natural numbers. There are lots of such problems which are unsolved. And these problems can, first of all, themselves be discovered. And once a problem has been discovered, we can then try to solve it – that is to say, to discover a proof of that problem. The very fact that a problem itself has to be discovered – and that there is ingenuity needed to discover a problem, and not only its proof – shows you that unintended consequences arise with the construction of the number system.

So the problems which we discover emerge as unintended consequences of our world 3 products. They are thus only indirectly the products of our minds. And this is the reason why I used the word 'roughly' when I said that world 3 consists roughly of the products of our minds.

I will call such inmates of world 3 – such as open problems which emerge from the world 3 itself without our doing anything, and which are beyond our control – 'autonomous' products. And I will say that world 3, though originating with ourselves, is very largely autonomous. There may be many autonomous problems, arguments, and theorems of which we know nothing as yet – and they may never be discovered by us.

This last point is decisively important, for it shows the following: although we started geometry and arithmetic (or number theory) ourselves, the problems and theorems may have existed before they were discovered by anybody. Thus they cannot possibly belong to the second world: they cannot possibly be mental states, subjective thoughts.

This establishes precisely what I call the 'autonomy' of world 3. The term is convenient though not important. What is important is the following statement.

> Although the various realms or regions of world 3 arise as human inventions, there also arise, as the unintended consequences of these inventions, autonomous problems and possible solutions to them. These exist independently of anybody's awareness of them: they can be discovered by us, in the same sense in which other things – say, new elementary particles or unknown mountains and rivers – can be discovered by us.

Now this means that we can get more out of world 3 than we ourselves put into it. There is a give and take between ourselves and world 3 in which we can take more than we ever give.

This holds for the arts as well as for the sciences. For it is fundamentally the same kind of give and take when a painter puts a speck of paint on his canvas and then steps back to look at the effect and to evaluate it. The effect may be intended or unintended. If unintended, the painter may correct or remove the speck of colour. But the unintended effect may also suggest to him a new idea: it may suggest to him, for example, a new balance of colours, more striking than the one originally aimed at. It may make him see his picture afresh, see different problems in his picture, see it in a different light as it were, and it may thus induce him to change his originally intended aim.

In a very similar way Einstein once said, 'My pencil is cleverer than I am.' What he meant, of course, was that by putting things down in writing and by calculating them on paper, he could often get results beyond what he had anticipated. We may say that by using pencil and paper he plugged himself into the third world of objective knowledge. He thus made his subjective ideas objective. And once these ideas were made objective, he could link them with other objective ideas, and thus reach remote and unintended consequences far transcending his starting point.

There is a moving story of the composer Joseph Haydn. In his old age he wrote *The Creation*. It was first performed in Vienna, in the

Aula of the old University of Vienna, a building that was destroyed during the Second World War. When he had listened to the marvellous introductory choir, he burst into tears and said, 'It was not I who wrote this. I could not have done it.' I think that every great work of art transcends the artist. In creating it, he interacts with his work: he constantly receives suggestions from his work, suggestions that point beyond what he originally intended. If he possesses the humility and the self-criticism to listen to these suggestions and to learn from them, then he will create a work that transcends his own personal powers.

You will see from this that my theory of world 3 leads to a view of human creation, and especially also of artistic creation, which is, at any rate, different from some very widely held views: from the view, for example, that art is self-expression or that the artist is inspired – though no longer by the Muses, the Greek goddesses of inspiration, but by his own physiological states, also called his 'unconscious', which has replaced the Muses.

These theories of art can be easily criticized on merely intellectual grounds as completely empty, quite apart from any such theory as the theory of world 3.

All this can be extended so as to cover quite generally the relation between a man and his work. And I will come back to it later. But at the moment I want to turn to a discussion of world 3 from the point of view of biological evolution.

I have tried so far to give a somewhat fuller intuitive picture of what I mean by 'world 3'. As far as objective knowledge is concerned, it may be said to be the world of libraries, of books and journals, but also of oral reports and oral traditions. Obviously, *language* plays a very great role in the third world of objective knowledge. But language also plays an important role in the arts. You will under-stand that I shall have to say much about language. So have most modern philosophers. But they are mostly interested in *words* and their *meanings*. I am not. I am interested in *theories* and the question of their *truth* – or their approximation or nearness to truth – and I regard words as unimportant. The situation may be represented by the following table:

Words	may formulate	Statements
	Table of the two sides of language	
Concepts or designations or terms		Propositions or theories or hypotheses or assertions
	They may be	
Meaningful		True
	and their	
Meaning		Truth
	may be reduced by way of	
Definitions		Derivations
	to that of	
Primitive concepts		Primitive propositions

Now my attitude to this table is as follows: although the two sides are completely analogous, the left-hand side is unimportant, while the right-hand side is all-important.

I may perhaps tell you that for a long time I was reluctant to publish anything about world 3. For a long time I did not even see that it can be characterized as the world of our products. I saw it just as the world of theories and arguments, and it all seemed so very abstract, philosophical, and vague. As I told you, I am allergic to hot air, and I did not feel confident that there was more to it than hot air. What made me feel more confident was the discovery that there is something analogous to the human world 3 even among the animals. This led me to a less airy view of the matter, and to a biological and evolutionary approach to world 3. And it led me to realize that, in a sense, world 3 is man-made – even though it is, in another sense, autonomous – and that it is in any case as real as world 1 since it can, through the intermediary action of world 2, act not only upon our minds, but also upon our bodies, and thus upon world 1.

It made me also realize that world 3 is all-important for the body–mind problem, and also for a theory of the human mind – a theory, that is to say, of its main characteristics, such as its selective consciousness, its selective memory, its enquiring attitude towards the world, and, ultimately, the ego, stretching through the past and expecting to have a future.

However, in beginning now to speak about evolution, I have to make a few general remarks. I am what may be called 'an admiring but reluctant Darwinian'. I greatly admire Darwin, and I regard the so-called 'modern synthesis of Darwinism' as a great step towards the truth. Yet at the same time I am well aware of the inherent difficulties and vagueness of Darwinism. It is far from being a satisfactory explanation of what happened, or of what will happen. But it gives some intuitive understanding, in spite of the many questions which it leaves open.

What I will mention first are some animal forerunners of our characteristic human proneness to evolve exosomatically through the creation of tools outside our bodies, and not only endosomatically through mutation and the evolution of new and better organs. As I said last time, instead of growing better eyes and ears we grow spectacles and hearing aids, and instead of growing faster legs we grow bicycles, motor cars, and aeroplanes.

Now there are also animals which produce exosomatic tools. I may mention spiders' webs, birds' nests, beavers' dams. But no animal other than man has produced anything like objective knowledge – objective problems, objective arguments, and objective theories.

Animals have produced languages. A bird's song, according to some modern theories, means 'Private property! Trespassers will be prosecuted!' This is also an exosomatic instrument and it has, like all animal instruments, an inborn genetic basis.

But animal *knowledge* is essentially endosomatic: it consists of inborn or acquired dispositions, and it is thus very much like human subjective knowledge.

It is clear that it must be a special characteristic of the human language which enables us to have exosomatic knowledge – knowledge which may be put outside ourselves and which thus may become *discussable, criticizable* knowledge. Our next problem will be to find this characteristic difference between animal language and human language.

DISCUSSION

Questioner 1: You said that you can make a discovery in world 3 in exactly the same way as, say, in the natural world. You said that to discover something in world 3 is exactly the same as discovering an unknown mountain or a river. I wonder if this is actually the case, or whether you are catching the significance of the fact that to validate a discovery in world 3 you have to produce an *a priori* necessary proof, whereas to validate a discovery in the natural world you just have to take somebody by the hand and point it out to him.

Popper: But I haven't. You see, a problem as such would be sufficient. Somebody says, 'Look here, it's very queer but what I draw here over this diameter looks like right angles. What could we do about it? They look like right angles, but I don't know whether they are or not.' Now, I am saying that this is to discover a problem. It's a problem in world 3. And the problem is: why are not all these triangles right angular? That's a problem, and the discovery of the problem is sufficient and he does not need to produce anything like a proof. If he makes a further discovery, it may be the discovery of a solution of the problem. That may be the proof. But I have spoken about the discovery of problems, and problems are as much inmates of world 3 as are arguments or theorems or proofs or whatever you may call them.

Questioner 1: I am not sure I would call that a discovery in world 3, but rather a discovery in the physical world. Because you have just asked me if I know the meaning of right angles. Only in terms of what they look like. If somebody has shown me something and says 'That's a right angle' and then he draws a circle with a diameter and so on....

Popper: I said that right angles belong to the things which we made ourselves in creating world 3. Only this problem about (you remember) my drawing – I've erased it. I'll make another one. We make a right angle according to a certain method, according to a certain procedure: we make a straight edge and a right angle. This is man-made. But the problem arises about right angles – about the relation of right angles and circles. At first sight circles and right angles are totally different things. But they are all related to the discovery, to a surprise. Also the problem *whether* they are related and *how* they are related is discovered.

35

Questioner 1: I am not questioning what you call the 'autonomy' of world 3 objects. Let me put it this way: what importance do you attach to a distinction made between necessary truth, which requires a discursive proof, and contingent truth which requires just attention to the fact?

Popper: If you don't mind I would suggest that we don't use too many technical terms in this discussion, which is more open than only for philosophy students and for mathematicians. Now, I would say, that whether a certain proposition is demonstrable or not is a world 3 problem. If it is demonstrable, then it's a world 3 problem to see what kind of proofs it gives. There may be several proofs. We may discover the proofs, the comparison of proofs – all these are things which are interesting for world 3. World 3 consists by no means only of necessary demonstrable propositions. It consists of all sorts of theories: physical theories which are not demonstrable – all sorts of things.

Of course, somehow or other the thing has to be started by us. For example, geometry has to be started by us, but once it gets going it produces its own problems. Physics has to be started by us, but once it gets going it produces its own problems. So it is with all the sciences. And so it is fundamentally with the arts. Somebody else can begin somehow to sing, or do something else musical before musical problems arise: the problem, for example, of how to end a piece – the problem of the cadenza, which may be one of the more obvious musical problems. I don't say, of course, that all these things are exactly the same. I did not say that we discover a problem in *exactly* the same way. Of course, if you think long enough, you can find some differences between the one and the other. I did say that we find a problem in the same way in which we find a mountain or a river, meaning by this that somehow we find something which is *there*. Of course, in finding it we are creative, and productive. I don't deny that. But still we discover a problem, and in a sense we cannot say that the problem was not there before we discovered it.

I shall speak about this question of time and world 3 when I have time to do so. But here the issue at stake is the *autonomy* of world 3, and you say that we should not quarrel about the fact that world 3 is, at least to a very considerable extent, autonomous – that is to say, that there are inmates in world 3 which nobody has ever thought of. Another very simple example can be given as follows. We put a mathematical problem into a computer, and sometimes the computer may solve it. Assume that the problem has been solved in the computer, and that the computer is so made that it can print the solution, and that the paper which it produces is at once put into the library and forgotten there. Nobody ever looks at it! There is a problem solved by a computer, and nobody ever looks at it! Of course the human mind was involved in devising the computer. But nobody knows *that* this particular problem has been solved, and nobody knows *how* it has been solved. It is just *there* to be found in the library for those who wish to find it.

Now this shows you, at any rate, that there are world 3 objects which are not really products of the human mind in the direct sense. Indirectly, yes. This I also admitted. Indirectly, by creating geometry we create geometrical problems. There is a difference here from the mountains, since indirectly it all goes back to us. But it goes back to us only indirectly, and the important thing is that we can get more out than we put in. This is why Einstein said, 'My pencil is cleverer than I am.' He can somehow get more out of world 3 than he put in. . . .

Questioner 2: Would you say that – given that the Babylonians invented the number system, and there are prime numbers as an unintended consequence, and there were prime numbers before the Greeks (or whoever) discovered them – would you not say that the number system was there *before* the Babylonians invented it?

Popper: I didn't say so. This is one of my main points. It is very important, and I intended to discuss it in a later part of my lecture. I think one has to accept this very interesting and serious world 3, but also one has to take away the hot air from it. And so we do up to a point by showing that there would not be such a thing if there were no human beings. And especially there would not be the Babylonians to invent it. I mean, there would not be such things as prime numbers if there had not been human beings who developed a number system. It need not really go so far, but it has to go up to a point in order to make the prime numbers. There would not be problems about prime number theory if we had not really invented the whole infinite sequence of numbers.

Questioner 3: So, when we create world 3 objects we *usually* create more than we are aware of?

Popper: Yes. And the main 'creator' here is language. Even the number system is fundamentally a linguistic affair. It is a linguistic method of finding new names for more and more and more real numbers. So language is really fundamental somehow to the whole thing. It is even very important in the arts. Even in the visual arts and also in music. But it is all-important in the field of the sciences. That is to say, in the field of objective knowledge – knowledge in the objective sense. And one of the things which I think is most reasonable to assume is that it is in the field of knowledge, rather than in the arts, that the human world 3 first blossoms out, and where the root of the matter lies. I shall also discuss this with you in evolutionary terms, as I promised to do.

Questioner 1: Sir Karl, this is basic for the same point that I raised before. I'm not so sure that you can say that the Babylonians invented rather than discovered the number system – because before the Babylonians you had a system of unit-counting. Now, there probably existed then a problem of how you are going to account for prime or 'higher' or 'prior' numbers, and wouldn't the solution of both decimal and other bases all have existed then if the Babylonians had discovered it? And couldn't unit-counting be said to exist – to have originated in the physical world, and therefore to have made world 3 dependent on world 1, rather than being a product of the mind?

Popper: This isn't right. The other point is excellent. There is no doubt that we usually find that a new invention is actually a solution to a previous problem. And so we can go back and back and back and always find that there was a previous problem. And to that extent it was more of a discovery than an invention. This is regarding the first point, and here we completely agree. There were obviously people who were unhappy about earlier number systems and found that there was a problem about how the invention of this method could actually be a solution to an earlier problem. And I suppose it can be found more generally elsewhere. But I don't see how you can come back to the physical world. I don't think that the physical world is, as such, ever a problem or an answer. Problems really are things which are connected with the *biological* world. There are problems for the survival of animals, not necessarily conscious ones. But you can say that an animal is adjusted to a certain environment and that when the environment changes there arises a problem of survival for the particular species. But I don't really see that problems arise before there arises animal life.

38

Questioner 1: But as soon as you have species existing, as soon as you have any being that can react to its environment, then the initial problems already exist. So the mere existence of, let us say, any animal and its environment would be the initial basis of the whole world 3, and everything will develop from that, every problem will develop from that. So it is not really dependent upon the mind, although the mind perceives the problems. But the problems exist whether or not the mind perceives them.

Popper: Yes, I would agree with that, but I will only point out that this evolution is itself by no means magic. That is to say, there may be very complex animals and never a world 3 in our sense: never a human language, never an argument, never these things which I have called specifically 'human'. But just these considerations which you have produced have led me – you remember, in connection with my first lecture – to approach the whole problem from a biological and evolutionary point of view.

Questioner 1: When you have an animal and you have a predator, and the animal sees its fellow species being eaten and runs away, you have a problem and a solution. Using your emphasis on evolution, I think you are going to find it hard to separate the human world 3 from the animal world 3. There's a continual evolution.

Popper: This aspect is still missing, but we will be able to do that too. This is a very interesting problem, and one which has something to do with the argumentative function of language. The whole question may be put under the heading of 'emergent evolution'. And of course this emergent evolution can be explained through this schema:

$$P_1 \rightarrow TT \rightarrow EE \rightarrow P_2$$

First of all, P_2 is different from P_1, and that is already something important to the matter. And second, you can say that the connection here is not one of determinism or causality. That is to say, it may happen differently. Whenever you have this schema, there are links in this which are anything but sure. You may remember that I said that a tentative theory on the animal level may consist of a mutation. This new mutation may come up or may not come up. A new theory may be invented. So wherever these errors are, there are loose points in between, and you do not find in the first animal everything which follows. And you can easily see this: there still survive animals which we know existed at a very early stage of animal evolution. Some of them have survived. Most of them did not survive. Why they survived or did not survive is very largely unknown and cannot be found out. New adaptations may disappear, others may not.

Questioner 1: I think I now know where I disagree with you. Although you have these numerous possibilities, I think that from the beginning all these possibilities existed and the only thing that may have changed is *which* of these possibilities have entered into our knowledge. All of them have existed in world 3. However, which theories or which tentative theories we use, and which new problems we came to, have just delimited what area of world 3 we can give to our knowledge.

Popper: I think we had better now stop this particular discussion because this raises quite new problems. And I would say: there is a *trivial* sense in which we can say that our possibilities exist, but this is only a very trivial sense. And the same applies to talking about all the possibilities which will ever arise, because we don't know in advance which of the possibilities *will* arise. This is the main answer to your question.

Questioner 4: As I understand world 3, man produces the rules of the game – the straight line, the circle, the right angle – and within these rules of the game there exists a sort of a logical relationship that man discovers. That's world 3. Would you say this is true?

Popper: Lots and lots of logical relationships, and some rules of the game, are very uninteresting and others turn out to be incredibly interesting and productive, and they lead to all sorts of discoveries. But otherwise I fully agree, as long as you realize that chess is less productive than geometry. Although it allows all sorts of combinations, it is less rich on combinations than geometry. And in application it is practically nil, while geometry is very rich in application.

Questioner 4: Take nature for instance. Here you have matter and energy. Now, are those two rules of the game? You have logical relations which are the rules of nature – how particles are moved such as this. Now, is this kind of rule of nature in any way connected with our sense of world 3? Is there any kind of logical necessity in nature...?

Popper: You speak about matter and energy. Now, these are human

40

concepts by which we describe nature. Of course there is something in nature corresponding to it, but you can't point to it. You can't separate it and say: *this* is matter and *this* is energy – it's impossible. Not only is that impossible but the particular chosen example of yours is unfortunate, because according to Einstein all matter is energy, somehow concentrated energy – so that you can't really distinguish between matter and energy. You can distinguish, let us say, between energy in the form of matter and energy in the form of radiation. Now, these things do happen, and these are human concepts. But we can point to things in nature which are energy in the form of matter, and other things which are energy in the form of radiation, and still other things which are both. Now, your question, as far as I understand it, is: 'How much of that is our invention and how much belongs to nature itself?' Is that the question?

Questioner 4: Actually, I should like to ask you if there is the same kind of logical necessity in world 3 as there is in world 1?

Popper: Logical necessity exists *only* in world 3. Logical connection, logical relations, logical necessities, logical incompatibility – all that exists *only* in world 3. So it exists in our *theories* about nature. In nature this does not exist, there is no such thing. . . .

Questioner 4: So world 3 and world 1 are sort of distinct?

Popper: They are *really* distinct, yes. World 2 intervenes between them. World 3 may have effects on world 1, and very great effects. Let us take the atomic bomb. This was entirely a world 3 invention. There wasn't such a thing in nature. One can show why there couldn't be such a thing in nature, because before the bomb is even assembled it would disintegrate – you understand. So, this was entirely a world 3 invention. And what kind of consequences it had not only on world 2 but also on world 1! So, world 3 has its effect on world 1, and a very strong effect – of course on world 2 also, but world 3 compared with world 2 is a tremendous amplifier of the powers of world 2 upon world 1. You understand? It makes a very much greater effect on world 1.

Questioner 5: I would like to ask Sir Karl about a very important truth: 'A thing is what it is and not another thing', to use Bishop Butler's statement in plain English. Now, when the young gentleman recently said, 'We invent the rules of the game' – I want to know first of all – 'A thing is what it is' – is that a rule? Did we invent it?

If we did, how do we account for its universality and logical necessity? And if it applies so closely to world 1 that Bishop Butler could state it – not as a tautology, and not as a logical truth, but sounding as though it were true about chairs, and even a truth about itself as an idea that we think in world 2 – how do we account for its necessity and its universality if we invented it, if it's a rule? Or, should it not rather be said to be a discovery? And if it *is* a discovery, is it a discovery *only* about logical necessity only in world 3? Is it not something that is also true about world 2 and world 1, and even about a fourth world? About any possible world?

Popper: I am not quite sure whether I understand you fully. You see, what I regard to be invented by us is language. Not that we invented it consciously. But it emerged somehow – especially human language, in which you can say such things as 'a thing is what it is'. That is part of human language – and we invented it. Now, it is part also of the evolution of human language that there arises something which we may call 'truth', and which we can describe. This is emphatically a world 3 affair. Already language is a world 3 affair – human language especially – and truth is even more a world 3 affair. Now truth, like other world 3 affairs, has a certain autonomy. That is to say, we cannot make a thing true by a stroke of the pen, as the dictators sometimes try to do, for example, by rewriting past history. We can't make these things true. So if I have understood you fully, that was really your question: 'Can we tamper with truth?' The answer is: of course we can, but then it is no longer truth. Truth is a circular concept like a proof, or the validity of a proof. Truth and the validity of argument are world 3 concepts, and we can call them by many different names, but nevertheless they are there in world 3. I may have to say this again in the lecture if I have time, but there is a very important thing here. The idea of objective truth *and* the idea of absolute truth – I will explain both – have become very unfashionable in certain circles, partly because people think they are presumptuous. And it *is* so. It *is* presumptuous to claim that we have objective truth or absolute truth in our pockets. I agree with this, but I would say that it is presumptuous *only* if we have objective truth and absolute truth: that we have not got them *in our pockets*, but they are somehow there *in world 3* – not in our pockets but in world 3 – otherwise it would not be presumptuous to say 'I have the objective truth and the absolute truth' (which one should never say). So, I would turn the tables on people who want to abandon objective truth, or absolute truth. Objective truth is pretty clear – it's just a world 3 concept. Absolute truth means the following. Some people say – and I have actually planned a lecture on this – some people say that there is no such thing as truth as such: only truth relative to certain assumptions, assumptions which then, in their turn, are not really true but are just accepted. I call this view 'the myth of the framework'. The myth of the framework takes several forms. For example, you cannot discuss a question without first assuming a framework. Against this, I assert that it's difficult sometimes to discuss a question if you haven't a common set of assumptions. It may be very difficult, but interesting and worth while. And out of these very difficulties arise real progress and new insight. So, so-called 'relative' as opposed to 'absolute' truth is the doctrine that all truth is only relative to a set of assumptions – that there is no such thing as truth which is not relative to a set of assumptions. This I turn down, and so I will turn down the myth of the framework with it. But objective truth is simply something in the objective world, so we can distinguish these two concepts. I don't know whether it is a sufficient answer at the moment.

Questioner 5: Tremendously helpful. Very true what you have answered.

Popper: Shall we stop or has anybody still a question ready?

Questioner 6: Sir, I have one question. I'd like to ask if world 3 is an autonomous world, and I just wondered whether you could turn it around and say that sometimes this autonomous world would assert itself into, say, world 2. For instance, in the dab of paint when the painter makes a mistake in one sense, and it suddenly opens up these possibilities – why couldn't we explain that by saying that world 3 had something to tell him and acted upon him?

Popper: That *is* what I am saying.

Questioner 6: That could happen? [laughter] Well, what would it feel like? How would you experience a thing like this? What other sort of analogous experience...?

Popper: I don't think that anybody who actually has ever worked on anything hard will have need for explanation. Let us say, if you write an essay for a tutor, or whatever it is, or for any purpose. Are you a student?

Questioner 6: Yes.

Popper: Now, I am quite sure everybody experiences it, when he really works hard on such a thing, that from the written work emerge new problems which he hasn't seen before. The essay can, when it works out, be even better than he ever intended or thought it would be when he had planned it. I think that is an experience which practically everybody has. I have it every day. Let us put it so: I don't know whether my lecture is very good, but it is certainly better than it was a few days ago, because I worked on it and tried to make it better. Now this doesn't come just from me. It comes from the interaction between me and what I have done here. I see that it creates certain difficulties which perhaps can be avoided, and so on, and be improved upon. The same happens with a composer. I don't know exactly how it is with very modern music, but with not so modern music it is very clear that the composer gets a very great deal from the medium – and not from the medium as such, but from the particular thing he has done, which suggests new possibilities to him. So I think this happens every day. It is one of my main points, that not only do we act upon world 3 but world 3 acts back on us. And it is actually – how shall I say it? I am almost preaching here – that I have a message here and the message is that modern theories of art, and indeed of work in general, have very much neglected this give and take between us and our world. Especially the theory that art is self-expression – a theory that is very widely accepted. This theory has completely forgotten that the artist may learn from his work constantly while he is creating.

Questioner 6: Then you could speak of 'plugging into' world 3. Is it possible for world 3 itself to initiate without man's initiating? Does world 3 – this autonomous world – could you ascribe to it an intention of its own?

Popper: I don't think so. I think there is a give *and* take necessary. Somehow we have to start, but we can, as I have said, get more back than we have put in.

Questioner 6: But man has to start it?

Popper: Somehow we have to start it. But there is no very great difficulty in that, because the starting of this can be shown to be genetically based. There is the innate ability and keenness to learn a language in every human being, which you can see particularly strongly and movingly in Helen Keller's description – you know of Helen Keller, who was deaf, dumb, and blind – of how she first learned the language. Everybody really should read that. There it is so very clear how much comes from *her*, because it's a give and take. Without her innate and, no doubt, genetically based capability for interpreting quite unnatural symbols as symbols, as names for water – it was water which ran into her hand and her teacher spelt the word 'water' into her hand. This link suddenly opened up the whole world of language and thought for her. Now, it is quite clear that if there were not a very strong need – a very strong and innate need and capacity for interpreting symbols, and an innate keenness to develop a language – then she would have found this attempt impossible. So it is already in us to develop a language, and with a language everybody participates in world 3 and contributes to it – you now, when you ask me, every man makes his contribution towards world 3 and gets something out of it. And usually he gets more out of it than he puts in. This is what happens to us all.

Questioner 5: Sir Karl, may I ask: would your world 3 have in it the possibility of discovery of moral structures? I want to ask the question in this way. In both early Hebrew writings and early Greek writings we find a symmetry between doing good to your friends and doing harm to your enemies. Or, as sometimes stated: 'Love your friends and hate your enemies.' And in both Hebrew thinking and Greek thinking there is criticism of this. Namely, that if we do hate our enemies and endeavour to do ill to them, then we ourselves become corrupt. And in both the Bible and in Plato you find a protest that there is no symmetry here – it is even said that it is bad to hate your enemies or to do ill to your enemies. Are these prophets of the Hebrew culture and philosophers of Greece discovering the same structure in the world 3 – so that there is some parallelism between a moral truth and, let us say, a logical truth such as 'A thing is what it is, and not another thing'? Does your world 3 admit of this possibility? You have often used illustrations from geometry, from the arts, but I notice no reference to the moral life in which we reflect on relations between men.

Popper: If you want such a reference you can find it in my *Open Society*, volume II – the 'Addendum' at the end of volume II tries to investigate this question. It is, of course, a very great question, a very difficult question. What I believe is that ethics or morals, or whatever you want to call it, is man-made, as is geometry, but produces its own problems, and the solutions of these problems lead then to further discovery. I do believe that there is a parallelism, and there is a good reason why I have not mentioned it here. I think, if it is going to be mentioned at all, it should be mentioned at a rather later stage. But it is even a question of – how shall I say? – at the moment you bring into any discussion like this the problems of morals and ethics, you, in a sense, make yourself suspect that you have an axe to grind – that you do the whole thing only because in the end you want to establish something ethical. Now, this I want to avoid. I want to make myself independent of this, and that is the reason why I did not mention it. But I do think that the situation is somewhat similar, and I also think – this is a question I have not yet discussed – that there is no finality in the moral field, just as in the field of science. It is all very difficult, but I don't think, for example, that there are such things as ultimate ideals or moral laws.

I think we are living in a world in which we have constantly to revise and constantly to think over not only our scientific propositions but also our moral attitudes. There arise new problems which cut right through what we have thought of as a generally accepted moral precept, and so on. There is give and take not only between ourselves and world 3, but especially between us and other people's situations which arise in the world. For all these reasons, I find it preferable not to say much about it in this particular course. Anyway if you want to see something about it, I would refer you to the 'Addendum' to the second volume of *The Open Society*.

3

WORLD 3
AND EMERGENT
EVOLUTION

Ladies and Gentlemen:

In my first lecture I explained to you the problem for whose solution I am trying to provide some ideas, the body–mind problem. I also told you of the main idea which I intended to use in the discussion of the body–mind problem: it is the idea of what I call 'world 3', the world of products of the human mind, such as a motor car, a skyscraper, a book or, most important, a problem and a theory.

World 3: products of the human mind (theories)
World 2: mental (conscious) experiences
World 1: physical objects, including organisms

I cannot sufficiently stress that I regard the products of the human mind as real: not only those which are themselves also physical – such as a skyscraper and a motor car, which everybody will call 'real' – but even a book or a theory. The theory itself, the abstract thing itself, I regard as real because we can interact with it – we can *produce* a theory – and because the theory can interact with us. This is *really* sufficient for regarding it as real. It can act upon us: we can grasp it, we can use it, and we can change the world with the help of the theory. I also told you of my intention to make use of biological and, more especially, of evolutionary considerations in trying to understand world 3, and especially that biologically most important region of it – knowledge in the objective sense – consisting in the main of theories.

In my second lecture I discussed in the main what I call the 'autonomy' of world 3.

By this I mean the fact that once we have started to produce something – a house, say – we are not free to continue as we like if

47

we do not wish to be killed by the roof falling in. Rather, there will be structural laws to be discovered by us, laws which we cannot change, and which are *autonomous*. So it is, I tried to show you, with geometry and with the theory of numbers. The relations between a right angle and a circle are unintended and unexpected. Prime numbers too are in no way under our control. They are unintended consequences of our invention of the infinite sequence of natural numbers. This invention, in its turn, may have been prompted by earlier problems with a limited sequence of numbers, and it may therefore have been more of a discovery than an invention. This, however, is not of great importance: the only reason why I stressed the difference between an invention and a discovery was that I wanted to explain to you the autonomy of the third world. For this purpose it is important to show that certain problems and relations are unintended consequences of our inventions, and that these problems and relations may therefore be said to be discovered by us, rather than invented: we do not invent prime numbers. But for most other purposes, the difference between invention and discovery should not be stressed: the two are very closely related, for every discovery is *like* an invention in that it contains an element of creative imagination. This also holds for the discovery of prime numbers.

My last remarks are prompted by the discussion we had after the last lecture, and I wish to take this opportunity to say how very good the two discussions have been which we have had so far. They were truly on a high level – indeed some of the best discussions I have had.

It was a great pleasure, but let us return to serious work.

I had originally planned to talk today about what I call 'the myth of the framework'. But all that has changed, and I now intend, first, to tell you a little about the reason why I feel that an evolutionary explanation of world 3 is important. To this end I shall try to tell you about the views of other people on those topics which I try to cover by the name 'world 3'.

Next I shall tell you a little about the theory of evolution, and about emergent evolution. This will be my second point.

My third point will be the evolution of human language from the level of animal language, and the reasons why the evolution of the specifically human functions of language is biologically significant. Here I will also discuss the peculiar role of objective knowledge.

My fourth and last point will be the emergence of the ideas or standards of true description and of valid argument – that is, truth in its objective sense, as opposed to truth in its subjective sense, which is equal to truthfulness or sincerity.

My own theory of world 3 has a long and interesting prehistory, which I do not, however, intend to treat in this course of lectures: it would lead us too far into details. Of the long list of names of philosophers who held some theory similar to world 3 – Hesiod, Xenophanes, Heraclitus, Parmenides; Plato, Aristotle, the Stoics, Plotinus; Leibniz, Bolzano, Frege; perhaps Husserl – I will mention only three: Plato, Bolzano, and Frege.

Plato believed in three worlds. His first world, the world which he said was the *only* world that was fully real – and indeed divine – corresponds to my third world. But it contained neither problems nor arguments nor theories. Roughly speaking, it consisted only of *concepts*, such as *Beauty* itself, or the *Good* itself. These he called 'Forms' or 'Ideas'. They were clearly meant to be objective, and visible to our intellectual intuition almost in the way in which physical things are visible to our eyes.

Plato's second world was the world of souls or minds, which was akin to his world of Forms or Ideas: before our birth, our souls lived in this world of Forms, and could see these Forms clearly. Our birth is a kind of fall from grace, a fall from which we enter the third world of physical bodies. This fall makes us forget our intuitive knowledge of the Forms or Ideas. But this knowledge can be partly recaptured by us, through philosophical training.

You will see the similarities and the differences between this and my own theory at a glance.

One difference is that Plato's theory is a theory of descent or degeneration – a theory of our fall – while mine is a theory of evolutionary ascent towards world 3. This difference is not unimportant. But it is by no means as important as the difference between the inmates of Plato's first world and my world 3.

Plato's first world consists of deified concepts, or of deified words. My third world, as far as its region of objective knowledge is concerned, consists of theories and, in addition, of open problems and of arguments.

Now you will remember that I gave you a table of the two sides of language. In this table we had:

Words		Statements
Concepts		Theories
	and their	
Meaning		Truth

About this I said that I regard the left side as unimportant and the right side as all-important.

Here is therefore the most important distinction between Plato's world and mine. Plato was the greatest of philosophers, but in putting in the foreground the left side of our table – that is, words, concepts, and meanings – he bedevilled the whole tradition of philosophy. Most philosophers, including the anti-Platonists (the so-called 'nominalists'), were under the sway of this tradition. And even the most recent philosophy, the philosophy of language analysis, or meaning analysis, is no exception: it is not a philosophy of language but a philosophy of words ('The New Way of Words'). It is not my intention to substantiate these allegations, although I shall be glad to do so in our discussion after the lecture. At the moment, all I wish to do is to point out similarities and differences.

The philosopher Bolzano populated what corresponds to my world 3 with 'statements in themselves' (*Sätze an sich*), as he called them. This was, from my point of view, a tremendous progress, as you will see when you remember the left- and right-hand sides of my table.

But Bolzano was greatly puzzled by the status of his world of statements in themselves. He suggested that this world was *real*, but indicated that it had not quite the same kind of reality as the physical world. And he could give no explanation of the relations between these worlds. These difficulties were felt the more strongly as he was an extremely clear and lucid writer. Accordingly, the impression was created that Bolzano's world of statements in themselves was not *really real*, but merely a figment or fiction of one philosopher's imagination.

Almost the same may be said about the philosopher Gottlob Frege. Frege remarked, in 1902, that we had to distinguish clearly between the psychological and the logical aspects of thought:

The psychological	*The logical*
Subjective thought *processes*, or acts of thinking, or thoughts in the subjective sense	Objective thought *contents*, or contents of acts of thinking, or thoughts in the objective sense

This was a very important remark. (But it remained almost isolated in his work until 1919, when, in a paper entitled 'The Thought: A Logical Inquiry', he introduced what he called 'the third realm' (*das dritte Reich*) – that is, the realm of thoughts in the objective sense.) Frege's third world, or 'third realm', consisted of concepts *and* of true and false propositions. But problems and arguments were not mentioned and did not seem to belong to it. Moreover, although Frege, like Bolzano, asserted that his third realm is real, he was hardly more successful than Bolzano in substantiating this claim. It is therefore not surprising that Frege's third realm did not win many friends. But it did win enemies who regarded it as mere fiction.

The list of the enemies of all these three world theories is very long. (It is even longer than that of their friends. The whole school of nominalists belongs to it, from Antisthenes on; also Descartes, Hobbes, Locke, Berkeley, Hume, and Mill; Russell's position is ambiguous, though he certainly believes in objective truth; and almost all students of language are opponents of third world theories, except a few such as Bühler, who is not too explicit. Hegel and Husserl fall into psychologism, and with them Dilthey and other *Geisteswissenschaftler*.)

I may remind you, especially, of the two strong monistic tendencies in modern philosophy which I mentioned in my first lecture. There are the philosophers of mind who try to reduce everything to mental states – insisting that, in the last instance, we know only of our own mental experiences. (As a recent and somewhat disguised 'linguistic' version of this view I mentioned the school that calls itself 'phenomenalism'.) And there are the materialistic, or physicalistic, or behaviourist philosophers, who claim that there exist *only* physical states – including the physical behaviour of people – and that it is an unnecessary complication to 'add' to these physical states the assumption that there are mental states also.

Both of these monistic schools agreed, of course, that adding a third world was preposterous, unnecessary, and fantastic. And with this, even the few surviving dualists – who believe in the first *and* second world – seem to agree.

Since you know that I am myself a pluralist who proposes the existence of (at least) three worlds, I need not dwell again on my disagreement with the monists. But I want to explain why for many years I did not say much about world 3, and why I used the name 'third world' in print for the first time only in 1966, even though in my publications ever since 1933–4 I had upheld a theory of knowledge which stressed the status of objective knowledge and the hopelessness of any attempt to reduce it to subjective knowledge.

My reluctance to write about world 3 was due to the fact that I am allergic not only to hot air but also to anything that resembles it or that is suspect of being associated with it. As long as I had no theory explaining the status of world 3 and its relation to world 2, I felt that it all sounded too much like a philosopher's fancy. (Bolzano's and Frege's theories did sound so to many other philosophers.)

Thus, I did not write explicitly about world 3 before I had found the simple, though somewhat 'rough', formulation that the objects belonging to world 3 are human products, exactly as honey is a product of the bees. And even then I did not use the name 'world 3' in print for another year, although I had often used it in seminars and lectures.

Two decisive insights encouraged me to take the plunge, since they made it abundantly clear to me at least that world 3 was not just hot air. First, the realization that world 3, though *autonomous*, was *man-made*; and that it was also fully *real*, since we could act upon it and could be acted upon by it: that there was a give and take, and a kind of feedback effect. And second, the insight that something closely analogous to world 3 existed already in the animal kingdom, and that the whole problem could therefore be surveyed in the light of evolutionary theory.

This brings me to the second point of today's lecture. I wish to make a few remarks about evolutionary theory in general.

There can be no doubt that Darwin's theory of evolution by natural selection is of the greatest importance. There can also be no doubt that this theory is, in many respects, in an unsatisfactory state.

There is a certain vagueness about this theory. For example, the theory operates with heredity *and* mutability – that is, with the facts that children resemble their parents in most points, not only because children and parents are human, but also beyond this: children also resemble their parents in individual traits. Yet they also differ somewhat from their parents, in most cases more and in others less. Thus the theory assumes, on the one hand, a high degree of stability of the hereditary material, and, on the other hand, a certain degree of mutability. Both assumptions are undoubtedly correct. But they allow us to explain, whenever convenient, some phenomenon as due to hereditary stability, and another as due to mutability. And this, in an explanation, is unsatisfactory, even when the assumptions are undoubtedly true. The unsatisfactoriness of the explanation lies in the fact that we can explain too much with this kind of assumption: almost everything that can happen, and even things which cannot happen. But if we explain too much, then our actual explanations become dubious.

Another weakness of the theory is this. Darwin tried to explain what we may call 'evolutionary ascent' – that is, the emergence, during long periods of time, of higher forms of organisms from lower forms. If we make use of Herbert Spencer's terminology and speak of 'the survival of the fittest', then Darwin's explanation may be briefly put like this: there is evolutionary ascent because, of all mutations or forms of life, only the fittest survive. But this will help as an explanation of evolutionary *ascent* only if we add a proposition like this: by and large, a higher form tends to be more fit than a lower form.

Yet this proposition – *by and large, a higher form tends to be more fit than a lower form* – is clearly untenable. In fact, we know that some of the lower forms have survived for very long periods – from a time long before the rise of the higher forms – and that these lower forms still survive. On the other hand, many of the higher forms which have risen long after the still surviving lower forms, and which survived for a considerable time, have disappeared. We do not know why, but it may well be that they were killed by bacteria or viruses – that is, by much lower forms. At any rate, these higher forms were less fit than many lower forms. These considerations show that a *close* connection between higher forms of life and fitness cannot be seriously upheld, and a very vague connection can hardly have much value as an explanation.

But the particular method of explanation by fitness is even worse. Biologists have long since felt that they cannot, as a rule, find out how fit a species is by inspecting it. They also cannot compare by inspection the fitness of two competing types. There is no other way to determine their fitness than to see which of the two competing types increases in numbers and which decreases.

But this means that biologists (especially Fisher) felt compelled to *define* as 'more fit' those which more often survive. Thus, what once looked like a promising explanatory theory becomes quite empty. The statement 'Evolution tends to produce higher forms because only the fittest survive' may sound like an explanation. But if we substitute here for 'the fittest' its defining phrase, we get: 'Evolution tends to produce higher forms because those forms which more often survive more often survive.' So our 'because' phrase has degenerated into a tautology. But a tautology cannot explain anything. All tautologies are equivalent to 'All tables are tables' or 'Those who live long are those who live long'. (Incidentally, this kind of degeneration happens frequently if we allow definitions to creep into our explanations.)

There also is no *predictive* force in any explanation by fitness. For if in the next generation a type so far surviving, or fit, does not survive any longer, then it was not fit for some of the new environmental conditions. These, of course, constantly change, since evolution itself changes them. It turns out, clearly, that fitness is always relative to existing conditions, and that we can say only, 'What is fit *here and now* is what survives *here and now*.'

I mention these points in order to make it clear that the theory is, to put it mildly, not entirely successful. It certainly cannot explain evolutionary ascent. What it can, perhaps, explain is an overall increase of *different* forms. And this it explains mainly by appealing to heredity *plus* mutability, which is a rather vague sort of explanation. In view of all this, it will hardly surprise you to hear that I regard the dreams of the eugenicists to improve the human population by genetic engineering as preposterous. Of course, I do not object to gentle measures designed to reduce hereditary diseases. But who is to judge what is good for mankind in the positive sense? Who is to be the judge of what will be better and better hereditary types? Who can foresee the conditions in which these types would be better types than others? The idea of letting some men meddle with mankind just because they have a smattering of genetics is too silly for words.

Having said all this, I want to say again that we have to be grateful to Darwin and his successors, for they have at least posed some extremely interesting problems. And they have given us the intuitive conviction that many important things can be explained only in terms of evolution. But there is obviously still much to be done in the field.

I now wish to offer you with the help of our old tetradic schema

$$P_1 \rightarrow TT \rightarrow EE \rightarrow P_2$$

a point of view which I hope may perhaps turn out to be a slight improvement on Darwinian theory.

I have originally explained to you the schema as a schema of the formation of theories: we start with problems, we put out tentative theories, then comes a process of critical error elimination or criticism, and then the new problem arises. At the moment I'll use this much more generally, in a much more general way – namely, as follows: I assert that all organisms are all the time problem-solving. They are faced with problems, and they are all the time problem-solving – even in your sleep you are problem-solving. When I stand quietly like this there are hundreds of muscles alive in my body which, by a kind of trial-and-error method and feedback, keep me from going too far left and from going too far right, and thus keep me straight. While I am apparently standing quietly, physiologists will tell you that, in reality, there is an immense amount of automatic piloting at work in my body to keep me on my straight course. Although I am not moving, but just standing quietly, nevertheless, all these things try to keep my balance. So this is the first thesis: all organisms are all the time problem-solving. So even a part of an organism is problem-solving.

You can, perhaps, explain this fact itself – that the organisms are problem-solving – by natural selection. That is to say, very early in the development, very early in the evolution of organisms, those organisms which were not problem-solving were eliminated. So now we have only problem-solving organisms.

Although I have put it first in a simple way – namely, that all organisms are problem-solving – I want actually to say much more.

If you remember the evolutionary tree, then one can distinguish what the biologists call 'phylum groups': families, genera, species, and individuals. I would say that each of these groups is problem-solving, and in solving their problems they all put forth TTs, and the TTs, the tentative trials, are very different at the different levels. I'll try to start with the individual. The individual itself constantly puts forth trials which it corrects by error elimination – not just human beings, but amoebae or bacteria and so on – and these trials are behavioural trials. The amoeba behaves in a certain way – each one extends pseudopodia, and so on – and all these behavioural movements are actually tentative trials put forth to solve some problem: sometimes feeding problems, sometimes escape from another animal, sometimes escape from another amoeba, and so on. So the individual organisms, in order to solve some problem, put forth tentative behaviour, and all of this is tentative, and underlies error elimination. And then you always have new problems. I'll discuss this a little more fully. But I want first to introduce a name – only for the sake of intuitive vividness – but I would say: *the 'spearheads' in the adaptation of the individual are the various behavioural patterns tried out by the individual.* The individual uses, so to speak, these behavioural patterns as its spearheads by which it tries, if you like, to conquer its environment, or to penetrate its environment, or whatever you like to call it. So behavioural patterns are the experiments, or the spearheads, or whatever you like to call it, put forth by the individual. Now in a similar way, the individuals are the spearheads – trial-and-error spearheads, or the tentative trials – used by the species. There is the species – something abstract, all the individuals of that species. But the species produces the individuals by mixing the hereditary material available to the species. It produces all sorts of tentative forms of individuals. This is, again, not fully random or accidental. I should have mentioned that the behavioural trials are not accidental or random, because very soon some are eliminated, and, also, they are always related to the solution of some definite problem, and this of course eliminates the randomness. Similarly with the production of the individual by the species. This again is not random, because certain genetic types are eliminated by natural selection or by other means. And therefore you have a large number of different individuals. And you can look at each of them, if you like, as a trial or a spearhead, or whatever you like to call it, used by the species to conquer its environment.

So I use, as a generalization of Darwin, the following ideas. First of all, we have not only struggled for life, struggled for survival. We have, also, concrete problems to solve. For example, the problem of keeping upright is not just a survival problem. If I sit down, I am not necessarily dead. I can survive. So my problem is quite different. Also, we can choose up to a point our various problems. The problem of standing up here would be one, and other problems that would go with my example just now would be in choosing how to sit up or how to stand up. But there are, of course, lots and lots of problems faced all the time by the various individuals, and these are behavioural problems. And there are lots and lots of problems of adaptation to the environment faced by the species, and it uses the spearheads, and the genes use the various species. If we come back to the main trunk of the evolutionary tree, we can see that all of these forms that evolution has developed are the present living spearheads trying somehow to penetrate the environment, the world, and even beyond the earth.

This is a generalization of the Darwinian idea that organisms have constantly to solve survival problems. According to my theory there are lots of problems which are not survival problems. When a tree puts out its roots, or arranges its foliage, it solves specific local problems posed by the stones and rocks in the earth and by the conditions of access to light. An organism may develop a preference for a certain kind of food, but may be able to survive on other kinds. To get the preferred food poses a problem. But it is not necessarily a survival problem. It may, for example, develop a preference for a certain food because, let us say, the food is easy of access or something like that.

Anyway, the preference may last even after the food is no longer easy of access. It was a new behavioural trait to prefer this kind of food, and this new behavioural trait may have developed and may have stayed even though the conditions under which such a trait was developed have changed. Now then, of course, the problem is a new problem for the organism. To get the preferred food poses a problem for the organism, especially if conditions change and the preferred food becomes less easily available. It can become a survival problem when the preferred food gets really scarce. In this case, it may be really a matter of life and death for these kinds of organisms whether they can get away from the preference or whether they keep to that preference.

Now, if the organism has difficulty in getting away from that preference, then we can say that it has developed a kind of *specialization*: it is specialized now for this food. This specialization may be a *tradition* (and if it is *only* a tradition, then the organism may get away from it) or it may have developed into a *genetic trait* – that is to say, it may have become a hereditary trait.

But what is really important for us in this theory is the following. The behavioural spearhead is, as it were, the real spearhead of the whole development. It is the real entrance where we try to penetrate. So behaviour is more important than anatomy. This is, I think, a point the biologists have missed. For an explanation of evolution, the main point is really the *behavioural* spearhead. Everything else follows this. Especially our preferences are decisive. Second point: if a behavioural trait or a behavioural specification lasts long – becomes a tradition – then there may be what I call a 'hereditary entrenchment' of this. This can be easily explained: as long as it is only a tradition, you don't really achieve perfection in your specialism, because you can always do other things too, and these possibilities interfere with the perfection of doing the one thing perfectly. But if it becomes hereditarily entrenched through mutations, then these mutations will do just that one thing which previously was done by tradition. And it will, therefore, develop it into a kind of perfection. So in the short run, or even in a fairly long run, the hereditary entrenchment of a specialization will have a survival value. And, therefore, for a considerable time, the hereditary entrenchment may really be superior and survive. But this hereditary entrenchment may turn out to be a death trap when the conditions change. Just because you can react only in a certain way, just because you can, say, eat only this kind of food, you will be lost when the food supply dries up. So the hereditary entrenchment of a certain trait may actually lead to the following interesting situation.

You can actually say – you can predict – that a certain very highly adapted species, very successful indeed, will actually die out at the next major change of environmental conditions, because it has become too specialized. So you can actually see into the future. And you don't know exactly when the conditions will change, but you can say that this organism is too specialized and actually too successful now, but that its success is misleading and that it will disappear at the first opportunity – that is, at the first big change in environmental conditions.

Now I have here a kind of summary that tries to show where I deviate from Darwin.

1   My problems are very specific. My problems are such as keeping in touch, or getting a certain kind of food, or similar, very specific, problems, whereas Darwin speaks, in the main, generally of survival.

2   The method of error elimination is not merely the struggle for survival between individuals, ending with the premature death of some of them. It also includes, for example, the avoidance of behaviour that was unsuccessful in achieving a specific aim.

3   A theory of the emergence of new forms is given: these are

explained as tentative solutions to emerging new problems. This is very important: the emergence of something really new, of a novelty.

Now we have seen already, in my first two lectures, that P_2 will be in general very different from P_1. We see from this particular schema that novelty can and must arise within evolution. So we have a theory of the emergence of new forms.

4 Systematic stress is laid on the leading role played in evolution by behaviour and by behavioural discoveries: behaviour is the real spearhead of evolution.

5 The role played by the development of new behavioural aims, preferences, and skills is stressed.

6 The role played by the broadening or narrowing of the spectrum of behavioural patterns, of behavioural possibilities, and by the broadening or narrowing of the genetic basis of behaviour is also stressed. Each plays a very different role, and – if you remember my earlier example – it does become a survival problem if a specific preference turns, through what I shall call a process of 'genetic specialization', or 'genetic entrenchment', into an inability of the race to survive on other than its preferred kind of food.

This simple example is very important, and we can learn a lot from it. So perhaps we should take a second look at it.

I will start, again, with the individual organism. Its almost unique genetic composition may be regarded as a problem-solving trial undertaken by the species, which brings forth a broad spectrum of different individuals, each with a somewhat different heredity or genetic composition. Each of these different individuals may be regarded as a *TT*, as a tentative trial. If a tentative trial proves unsuccessful and is eliminated, the probability of a new trial with a similar genetic composition will be somewhat reduced. This is still Darwinism (or, as it is now often called, 'the new synthesis'). We can say that the species used the individual organism as a spearhead in trying to penetrate, or conquer, its environment.

We can next look at the behaviour of the individual organism. Behaviour is partly determined by heredity – that is, by genetic composition. But it will have a certain range or spectrum: there will be different possible behavioural reactions at the individual's dis-posal in similar or different problem situations. Each of these behavioural reactions may be considered as a *TT*. And the individual organism may learn, by error elimination, how to solve its problems – in our example, how to get the preferred food. So behaviour is a spearhead of the individual organism, and so we have:

Behaviour: Individual = Individual: Species

But the development by the individual, or by a number of individuals, of a preference for one kind of food was also a behavioural solution to a certain problem situation. This preference may have been adopted simply because of the relative abundance of that kind of food, or for many other reasons. It is, however, crucial whether the preference is maintained by tradition or becomes hereditarily entrenched.

I will speak of a tradition as a behavioural pattern which does not change over a considerable period of time, *although other behavioural patterns or solutions are available from the point of view of the genetic composition of the organism.* And I will say that a way of behaving has become genetically or hereditarily entrenched *if no other patterns are available* – that is, if the type of organism has become genetically specialized.

Specialization may thus be a matter of a tradition that can be broken, or of a hereditary entrenchment that cannot – since heredity is not dependent on the individual's behaviour, while the behaviour may more or less rigidly depend on heredity.

Turning now to our tetradic problem-solving schema, I may sum up. Let us look at the genetic tree.

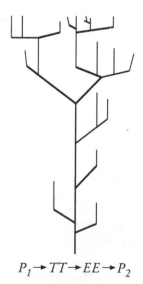

Individuals or species or genera or phyla – they are all the time unconsciously solving problems. The behaviour, or perhaps the tradition, is the TT or spearhead of the individual. The individuals, in turn, are the TTs or spearheads of the species or race. The species is the TT or the spearhead of the genus. And so on.

$$P_1 \to TT \to EE \to P_2$$

3. WORLD 3 AND EMERGENT EVOLUTION

I turn now to a new problem: *a behavioural tradition may also become the spearhead of a genetic entrenchment – that is, of a genetic change in the species of the race.*

This genetic entrenchment of what has been previously a tradition can be comparatively easily explained – for a fairly rigid behavioural pattern due to a tradition will be, as a rule, slightly less successful than a (perhaps still more rigid but otherwise precisely similar) pattern due to genetic specialization. This is simply due to the fact that specialization is carried a step further: as long as different patterns of behaviour are still possible to the individual, these possibilities interfere slightly with the perfection of the behaviour. Now the increase in efficiency makes it probable that mutants which happen to entrench the behaviour genetically will be successful. Mutants which specialize for the favourite food may have an advantage, for the time being, over non-specialized types. So the genetic composition of the species may change, and the frequency of mutant types may increase in the population until a reversal becomes impossible or difficult or too slow to save the species from extinction. This kind of entrenchment is a well-known hereditary mechanism. What may be new is the thesis that this mechanism, though highly successful as a rule, is a very dangerous affair. In fact, it is a kind of death trap for the species. Although the species may in this way become more successful or 'fitter to survive', it is bound to become unfit at the next relevant change of environmental conditions – for example, when a highly specialized food supply dries up.

Thus, although I do not, in my theory, have an idea of fitness which can be used for prediction, I do have an idea of *unfitness* which can, indeed, be used for long-range prediction. It is simply this: *every genetic entrenchment of a specialization is bound to be lethal in time, even though it may be extremely successful for the time being, and perhaps for a long time to come.*

The opposite cases of genetically entrenched specialization are species with a broad spectrum of possible behaviour patterns. Although their outlook seems rosier, we cannot predict anything about their future, since there are always many unforeseeable changes possible (the evolution of a new virus, for example) which may be fatal for the species. A good example is the cedars of Lebanon. They were well adapted and fit – until man developed the world 3 plan to utilize their fitness for ship-building. This practically exterminated them.

How does the old Darwinian problem of genetic ascent look from the point of view of this theory? First, it becomes clear that it is wrongly put. There is no such thing as a general genetic *ascent*. There is such a thing as a tendency towards increased *variety*, towards more and more different species, as new problems emerge and are solved, leading again to new problems. So we should, perhaps, draw the trees horizontally:

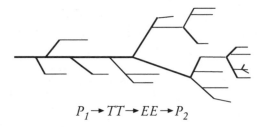

$$P_1 \rightarrow TT \rightarrow EE \rightarrow P_2$$

Our tetradic schema makes it clear that the new problems will in general depend only very loosely upon the old ones: the tentative solutions create a new situation. In addition, the external conditions may change, owing to the change in other species or in the physical environment.

This looseness of the connection means that a new problem can be really *new*, in the sense that there never existed anything like it before. Thus our tetradic schema makes the emergence of novelty comprehensible. The term 'emergent evolution', which usually has been regarded by critical thinkers as belonging to the category of hot-air terms, may be said to have become perfectly cool and solid because of our theory and because of our tetradic schema. For instead of a mere *term*, we have now a *theory* of emergent evolution.

Instead of speaking of higher organisms, we may speak of more complex organisms. And an increase in complexity may be understood as a consequence of increased variety, explicable in terms of our theory of emergence.

It is quite clear that increased complexity, as such, has nothing whatever to do with fitness or unfitness. For any really catastrophic change of the environment, such as a collision with a really big meteorite, while bound to destroy all complex organisms within the region, may well allow many simple organisms to survive.

Now I had, as you know, planned to do more in this lecture. But it is getting somewhat late, and we should perhaps leave the evolution of human language and the emergence of the ideas of truth and validity for next time. But to sum up again, our theory – based upon our tetradic schema – is a theory of emergent evolution through problem-solving. The emergence of evolutionary novelty is explained by the emergence of new problems. The theory regards all organisms and species (and even all phyla) as constantly engaged in problem-solving. The problems are solved on various levels: the individual invents new behavioural patterns by the method of trial and error elimination; the race or phylum invents, as it were, new individuals by inventing new genetic patterns, which are new genetic compositions, including new mutations.

In a changing world, it will be advantageous for the species if its evolution has a broad genetic basis, permitting a broad spectrum of differently endowed individuals and a broad spectrum of behaviour.

This broadening may sometimes be achieved by the invention of new preferences and new aims, more specific than mere survival. (See my Spencer Lecture.) Yet such new aims may also lead to a narrowing of the possibilities of hereditary behaviour through specialization.

Some deviations from Darwinism are the following. (1) The new problem may be quite specific and may be linked only loosely to problems of survival. (2) The method of error elimination is not merely the struggle for survival between individuals, but includes, for example, the avoidance of behaviour which was unsuccessful in achieving a specific aim. (3) A theory of the emergence of new forms is given: new forms are explained as tentative solutions to the emerging new problems. (4) Systematic stress is laid on the leading role played in evolution by behaviour and by behavioural discoveries: behaviour is the real spearhead of evolution. (5) The role played in evolution by the development of new behavioural aims, preferences, and skills is stressed. (6) The role played in evolution by the broadening or narrowing of the spectrum of behavioural patterns, and by the broadening or narrowing of the genetic basis of behaviour, is also stressed.

DISCUSSION

Questioner 1: If I have understood your $P_1 \to TT \to EE \to P_2$ schema correctly, Sir Karl, you maintain that problems may arise both from TT and from EE. Now I see how problems may arise from TT, that this tentative theory may itself be problematic and require testing and error elimination. But after testing and error elimination – I don't quite see that error elimination also leads to a new problem. That you didn't cover.

Popper: The problems come from both places, from both *TT* and *EE*. But you see, the error elimination, of course, leads to a new problem itself. If an error in this *TT* is eliminated, then this P_1 and this *TT* disappear, and a new problem arises which is not the old problem. That is to say, we have now at least the advantage that we know, or the organism knows, that this *TT* isn't a solution. Therefore we are in a new problem situation. The original problem permitted this as a solution. The error elimination eliminates that. Therefore, a new problem arises, namely: to try to solve the problem, but not in this way. This is a new problem, if the error elimination is contradicted. . . .

Questioner 1: Perhaps I and others, Sir Karl, cannot be so sure about that, because you illustrated *TT* rather more fully than *EE*. Isn't that correct? You didn't give examples of *EE* as fully as you gave examples of *TT*.

Popper: Oh yes, a typical example of error elimination would be, for example, if *TT* was an entrenched preference for a certain food – but even if it is not entrenched – if it is a preference for a certain food and the food dries up, then the drying up of the food actually means that this *TT* was an *error*. So this will be eliminated, and the new problem arises, and this will no longer be the solution. So, I think this is pretty clear.

Questioner 2: Is it too early to use that as a metaphor for human culture – when you said that new forms must necessarily arise in P_2? Are you saying that in human society or human culture new forms necessarily must occur? Can I use that metaphor, or is it only . . .?

Popper: I wouldn't say necessarily, but otherwise it's all right. New forms do emerge, but we don't know when and how. So the 'necessarily' should be rather taken. . . .

Questioner 2: One reason I ask that, Sir Karl, is, did you see Ernst Gombrich's review of Erich Kahler's *Disintegration of Form*? He used your name in vain, I hope, saying – somewhat agreeing with Kahler – that one could give a qualitative judgement of new forms, and it seems to me in this you are not implying any kind of qualitative judgement.

Popper: I do not really understand your question. Could you explain it so that everybody understands it?

Questioner 2: I have to mention Kahler's book *Disintegration of Form*, because he says that modern society – modern art mainly – is a reflection of the disintegration of values. And Gombrich in his review of the book agrees with that, using you, and I forget exactly how. But in looking at this metaphor, I do not see any implication that there is a qualitative change in new forms arising in the P_2 category. I'm asking, is there a moment when that happens?

Popper: There *is* a qualitative change very often. The point is really this: P_1 and P_2 are very often very loosely related, and this looseness between the relation of P_1 and P_2 explains the novelty of P_2 up to a point, and therefore its emergence. And its emergence means that something completely and qualitatively different may arise in this process. The best example of this is to look at the evolution of science. After each structural change in scientific theory the problems look utterly different. Remember for example the problem: is the earth in the centre or is the sun in the centre? We have gone very far beyond this. Our problems are very urgent, but do not in the least resemble this particular problem any longer. But they have emerged, of course, from this problem. Who asks today what is in the centre of the universe? To say nothing about earth and sun and so on – the whole problem no longer arises. So, let us say, instead of such a problem we have at present perhaps such problems as whether we can observe with our terrestrial means the rotation of our own galaxy. That is the nearest problem which is similar to this old problem, and completely different. Nobody asks whether our own galaxy is in the centre, for example. But the problem whether the galaxy rotates, and in which way it rotates relative to the other galaxies, of course – this problem is an existing problem and the nearest I can think of. But how utterly and in every respect different it is. The centre does not arise any longer, and instead of it, something like rotation, which has nothing to do with whether it is in the centre or not. So it is a real qualitative change altogether. That is something which I have just at the moment thought of as an answer to this particular question. I don't think it is necessarily a very good answer, but the best examples are always from the evolution of science, because they are the most concrete ones.

Questioner 3: I don't entirely understand, Sir Karl, your criticism of Darwin. I agree with your criticism of Spencer, who, I think, misrepresented Darwin, but I don't understand your criticism of Darwin at all. In the first place, it seems to me that Darwin is not about the business of explaining evolutionary ascent except in the case of man. He is more often in the course of his writing, very much more often, in the business of explaining why one finds different forms in different ecological niches – which is an entirely different problem from describing evolutionary ascent.

Popper: I can't quite agree with your general description of Darwin's problems – these problems you say Darwin had. But what he really, ultimately wanted to explain is this. It is very clear. It was quite often said that the problem Darwin left over was the origin of life. Once you give him that, he tries to explain evolutionary. . . .

Questioner 3: I think his grandfather was interested in that problem, because, you know, Erasmus Darwin thought everything came from a single living element. But it is not my impression that Charles Darwin was as interested in that problem. I was not quite sure why you wanted to attack him on that ground. It's not really a question of whether lower forms still exist, because a lower form, given its place in the general scheme of ecology, might very well survive only because it *is* a lower form of life, or because it is perfectly adapted to the conditions which it would normally encounter.

Popper: Yes, but you see, if that were so – but the point is really – when I speak about Darwin, incidentally, I mean partly what is usually now called 'Darwinism' – namely, what Huxley has called 'the new synthesis', and what the now fashionable biologists call 'the new synthesis'. It goes back to this book of Huxley's which you probably know. I should really have said this, that when I speak of Darwin I mean what has been called until a few years ago 'neo-Darwinism' and is now called 'the new synthesis'.

Questioner 3: That's a very different thing. OK.

Popper: As to the ecological niche. You see, the very queer thing about some lower organisms is that their ecological niche is almost unlimited. You may see that from the discussion, about which probably most of you have heard, of the infection of planets and the moon and stars when they are reached by American or Russian spaceships. One is afraid that the Russians may not be sufficiently cautious with regard to infection. Now what does it all mean? It means that we attribute to some lower organisms almost universal adaptability. They can live under the most severe and under the most extreme conditions. We can, only if we put spaceships round us. But these lower organisms have practically no ecological niche, and we trust that they can live anywhere and everywhere. It's also very interesting. . . .

Questioner 3: That may be just a simple mistake.

Popper: It is *not* a mistake. We have found that they can live and survive even if they are frozen and dried up. They can live almost indefinitely under the most extreme conditions. It wouldn't be a mistake to say that if they get stuck in this shape on a spaceship they may perfectly well survive the flight. That is not a mistake. It's quite possible. And that is the reason why this particular problem has been discussed recently.

Questioner 3: Well, the reason I say it may be a mistake is because it will not be the same organism. I'm thinking, for instance, specifically about certain types of bacilli which have been eliminated for scientific purposes in highly antiseptic conditions, but which have produced different strains which are able to survive. However, that is not the same organism, and it is very much the same as your P_1–P_2 thing.

Popper: It is an organism which may produce the old organism, and to that extent it is not entirely a new organism. It has the memory that it is also the old organism. It really doesn't matter. If you take a bacterium, then it never dies normally because it doesn't produce offspring and then die, but it produces offspring by splitting itself. So, if you take a present-day bacterium, none of its ancestors has died. In other words, it's still the same 'thing' as the original bacterium from which it comes. So we could say the very opposite of what you say: it is not a new organism but a very old organism in a slightly changed form. An extremely old organism – I mean as old as organisms are. The problem of individuality is different for bacteria. And there are all sorts of aspects to this, but the main point in all this is the following. Some people have tried to say: 'Look at Man!' They have objective criteria – biological criteria, not ethical – biological criteria why man is the highest of organisms. Obviously, man is able to adjust himself to all sorts of circumstances to which no other organisms can adjust, except the very lowest ones. So it's no criterion of complexity that you can adjust yourself to all sorts of things. I'm speaking about biological criteria. Next time I will give some other criteria with the help of world 3. But biological criteria by which we can say that certain organisms are higher than others do not, I think, exist. We can say that they are more complex, but greater complexity may be connected with anything you like – with unfitness, and so on. I mean, when an organism becomes very complex then, for example, almost every gene mutation – that means almost every mutation – is lethal. Because of the complexity of the organism, any sort of imbalance brought about by mutation will be lethal. That is to say, the vast majority of all mutations *are* lethal. What you have described about change of the organism shows the greater changeability of the lower organisms, because they are not so complex. So complexity, from a biological point of view, is a very great disadvantage, and not necessarily an advantage at all. It depends on where the complexity leads us. I don't say that complexity is bad, or anything like that, of course. But I mean it is not *in itself* an advantage. So, I had in my lecture, you remember, a little diagram in which I take my evolutionary tree, and put it horizontal instead of vertical, and put it like this, and say: all we have here is increased diversity which, among other things, means also new complexity. You start with simple things, and the simple things survive. But in addition to them, you also get complex things. So we get increased diversity, but not higher and higher. This, I think, is an objective statement, while to speak of evolution of higher forms means, I think, bringing in a kind of anthropomorphism. Now I do think that the anthropomorphism may be justifiable. But it is not a *biological* idea. I mean, to be anthropomorphic and see man somehow as the highest animal may be justifiable, but it's not necessarily a biological idea. When, for example, the idea was – not very long ago and it is still not dead – the idea was very much alive that life might have been brought to earth by infections through meteorites. This idea was very much alive about, let us say, one hundred years ago – or a little less, seventy years ago. It isn't very much alive now, but still even today meteorites are investigated from this point of view too. Opinion is divided on whether or not they do bring some infection onto earth. So this shows that we do attribute to lower forms of life a quite tremendous possible range, a range beyond the human reach at present. Possibly we may one day compete with them in that respect. But they do it in a simpler way, if they do it at all. Their method is much simpler than ours, and not so dependent, let us say, on the supply of special skills and such things, and of very much money, of lots of money.

Questioner 4: I wonder, would you level the same criticism at the Darwinian thesis or hypothesis or whatever you want to say – that it isn't satisfactory because it explains too much? Would you apply the same criticisms to field theory, or to the general or special theory of relativity, or to any other such specified theory?

Popper: Oh no!

Questioner 4: How would you distinguish between why you wouldn't in one case and you would in the other?

Popper: Because the predictions made by Einstein's theory are very precise. You cannot make *any* predictions with the help of evolutionary theories so far. Now, I think one advantage of my theory is that there is, at least, some prediction in it – namely, the prediction that while hereditarily entrenched specialization may at the moment be as successful as you like, it is somehow bound to disappear if conditions change. And there is also a theory of how this hereditary specialization arises. Moreover, there are a few other predictions in my form of the theory, but I can't really now go back to it all. The main thing in my form of the theory is that mutations can succeed only if they fall in with an already established behavioural pattern. That is to say, what comes before the mutation is a behavioural change, and the mutation comes afterwards. And this is testable, and so far a prediction in principle. I will give you an example – I think one should really make this concrete – a very good example is the evolution of a woodpecker's beak and tongue. Ask yourself what has come first, a change of taste or a change of anatomy, and you will see at once that if a change of anatomy had come before a change of taste, the woodpecker would not have known what to do with its new outfit. The new outfit would have been lethal. But if a change of taste for a new kind of food comes first, and if a woodpecker, because of a change, pecks the wood long before it has a beak, then mutations which help it to peck the wood more easily – more efficiently – these mutations will at once be selected. I think this can be put quite generally, and it actually can be put in this way. What leads in evolution is behaviour. And what leads in behaviour are *new aims*, and next new skills, and only in the third instance is there an anatomic change. The anatomic change comes only afterwards, but

69

what comes first is behaviour, and this partly explains also evolutionary tendencies. So there is quite a lot in this theory that is testable. I don't know whether my theory is true but I think it is testable.

Questioner 5: How does that differ from what Lamarck said?

Popper: I have somewhere written in a lecture, in the Herbert Spencer lecture I gave in Oxford some years ago, there I said that the problem is that with almost every sequence of theories, a new theory has to simulate the old theory. The new theory simulates the old theory, so, in a way, Darwinian theory simulates the Lamarckian effects. Already the Darwinian theory – roughly speaking, we get Lamarck explained by Darwin in this way. The difference, however, is very great, because according to my theory and Darwin's theory, Lamarckism is wrong in so far as behavioural traits are not inherited. They only stimulate a *selection pattern*, not the inheritance as such, but a selection pattern. That is to say, what the behaviour does is create a new ecological niche! A new behaviour creates a new ecological niche, and then the selection pressure operates so that this niche is filled. Again it is only a simulation of Lamarck and not a Lamarckian theory. That is really the decisive point in the whole thing. You have to simulate Lamarck's theory, but it is a question of how you do it.

One point of my theory can be directly put like this – it is, of course, an oversimplification, and it says only by and large – but by and large, new aims come first, new skills come second, new traditions come third: and then you have created a biological niche which is filled by selection pressures. And that is very dangerous.

Questioner 6: When you speak of these new aims – these new behaviour patterns – where do they come from? What motivates them?

Popper: From the schema: $P_1 \rightarrow TT \rightarrow EE \rightarrow P_2$.

Questioner 6: I mean are they conscious – the new aim, say, of a woodpecker?

Popper: Conscious? About consciousness I shall speak in the lecture after the next. But to put it roughly: I do think there are lots and lots of degrees of consciousness, and we can observe that in ourselves. A dream is in a different way conscious from your consciousness when you are awake, but it is certainly conscious. But it is conscious in a very different sense. For example, in a dream we hardly ever have an organized memory: we have neither a dream memory, nor a real memory, but *no memory* – although the dream is supplied by memory. But you don't dream that you remember something – or perhaps you do, but very rarely. Extremely rarely. In a dream you are in a different relation to space and time from when you are awake – completely different in relation to space and time and especially, as I will point out when I come to discuss consciousness, the relation to time is terribly important in the higher forms of consciousness. It is probably completely absent in the lower forms of consciousness. So there is probably an almost unlimited number of degrees of consciousness. And whether lower animals are conscious or not is very difficult to say. Jennings, who has written this book on the behaviour of lower animals, gives very many vivid illustrations, for example, of chases between amoebae in which it is almost impossible to deny that the amoeba is, in some sense, conscious – but surely not exactly in our sense. Very difficult. We don't know anything about the consciousness of animals. We can only take a sort of impression-istic approach to this particular question. I don't say that the approach is useless. So this question I don't want to answer. But I do want to say that one can say a lot more about the schema. And I do want to say that the schema does explain to you novelty in many ways. I'll give you one way: the creation of any new *TT* changes the whole situation. Apart from that, the situation itself changes because there are other animals with which you interact. The environment constantly changes – if for no other reason, then because the sun-spot cycle changes. It may start from there. Weather changes, all sorts of things change. But certainly we ourselves change our conditions through adaptation, and thereby change everything, all the time. So there are constant changes, and the ways in which these changes go we cannot predict. It means that P_1 and P_2 are very loosely connected, and that means that novelty emerges. Earlier, I said quite a bit about this particular problem – namely, that the idea of emergent evolution was always a bit suspect to scientists. One always felt 'emergence' was a very vague concept. Now, this schema really gives it a definite meaning, or a definite point. It allows us to explain why novelty arises – or emerges if you like – and thereby we can really say that emergent evolution is on a more solid basis than it has been without such a schema. It was always terribly difficult to see that something entirely new can arise. All right, you always have mutations. But if you actually look at works on mutations, you will find this very disappointing, because the same mutations always arise. In most experiments with *Drosophila*, which is the main organism used for getting mutations, there are all sorts of very well-known mutations which come up again and again and again – and these well-known mutations have names. And in the end you have the feeling: how can anything new arise through mutation? So mutations are somehow unsatisfactory as means of explaining anything new. You can only say, 'Oh yes, in time there will be new mutations', and similar things. But if you do point out *why* there is a change of circumstances – which may be systematic, especially if you have a new aim – you see, the new aim then makes the change of everything systematic. That is pretty clear, isn't it? Let us say, if you have a new aim because of a new food preference, then the selection pressure now will be systematized, and therefore the mutations will really be an advantage. One good example was the woodpecker. One has often asked how it is that these big mutations are all lethal. How is it that these very small mutations which, we have to postulate, have no lethal effects – how is it that these small mutations may effect bigger changes? The answer is: only if there is a systematic selection pressure. Now, this selection pressure may be due to an environmental change, or it may be due to new aims. But even in an environmental change, it will only work if you quickly develop new aims. A biologist with whom I had a talk a few days ago gave a very good example, namely: how did the fish get legs? The answer: when certain parts of the sea were drying up, they had to try and move from one little pool to another pool, and some still do so. All right, there was an environmental change. But the decisive thing was that they responded to this with an *aim* – namely, the aim to get to another pool. Those who did not respond with that aim were probably eliminated. Those that did respond with the aim had a *new* aim. And with that new aim, the slightest improvement in transport on land – with every element of improvement – would at once be a great new addition. So very small changes can now begin to add up, but only if the reaction to the big environmental change is a behavioural change, and only if the behavioural change is of the type of a new aim. Of course, that may develop out of an accidental behaviour of trial and error, but anyway it happens in that way.

Questioner 7: Sir Karl, may I ask if this formula is complete? Wouldn't it be better, rather than to think of the first problem P_1 and then P_2, to go somewhere in the middle and to have P_M and P_N and P_O?

Popper: I have actually written down in the first lecture something like that. I can show you. I had it on the blackboard.

Questioner 8: Then this was an oversimplification?

Popper: Of course! I said it there. It *is* an oversimplification, but it is sufficient to show the emergence of novelty.

Questioner 8: But you have talked about problems and not at all about pseudo-problems. And I would like to ask whether the concept 'pseudo-problem' has not been much too simple? Whether 'pseudo-problem' has not been used in an absolute way when it should always be used in a relative way? And whether your formula is not most suggestive because if, let us say, P_M is a problem at T_M, then P_N, which you haven't yet come to, is in that relative sense a pseudo-problem – and whether from T_O, when P_O is your problem, P_M and P_N are not also pseudo-problems? Now an anachronism then has two senses temporally: it's either an old problem that you are past, or it's a new problem that you haven't yet come to. Or another form of relativity, since we are talking about organisms always in an environment, is that a pseudo-problem for an organism in one environment may be a real problem for some other organism in that environment, or for some similar kind of organism in a different environment?

Popper: There are two different things here. I broadly agree with you, but I have not had time to develop the problem of problems – I mean the problem of different kinds of problems, especially of different senses. Namely, the sense of 'problem' in which I was speaking about biological evolution is – we humans look at those poor animals and see what their problem was. Of course the animal had no idea what its problem was. We can use the term 'problem' – the animal can't. How is it with the scientists? It turns out to be very similar. A scientist may actually deal with a problem and solve a problem and it may turn out that *ex post facto* – after the event – we see that actually the problem that interested the scientist was quite a different one. I have one very good example, that of Schrödinger. There are many other examples, and I will give you another one later. Schrödinger tried to solve a problem which was roughly this: how could we give a continuity theory of quantum mechanics? A theory in terms of continuity mathematics? That was more or less his problem, and that was solved by wave mechanics. Then a few years later – two years later, after Schrödinger wrote his various papers on wave mechanics – Max Born gave an interpretation of it. What Schrödinger had regarded as a continuous distribution of electric charge was now interpreted as the probability of finding an electron in a certain place. What was continually distributed was no longer the electric charge, but the *probability* of having an electric charge somewhere – namely, an electron – and the electrons were of course *discontinuous rather than continuous*. So Schrödinger's problem had disappeared somewhere, and we can say now that Schrödinger solved a problem of whose existence he did not know – namely, the problem of the probability of an electron being at a given place. But of course this problem was only discovered by Born after the event, and Schrödinger never intended to solve this particular problem.

Now a very similar example is Kepler. Kepler tried to solve the problem of the harmony of the world. Actually he did quite a lot towards it, and all the things he said are extremely interesting. But we say nowadays that he solved the problem of Kepler's laws. Just a hint of how little this was his own problem is the following. The second of Kepler's laws asserts that the radius vector – that is the line between the sun and a planet – sweeps over equal areas in equal times. Now, if you draw an ellipse – here is the sun and here is the planet – you will see that the further the planet is away from the sun – that is, if the planet moved with more or less constant velocity, the radius vector would sweep over much wider areas if the planet was away from the sun than if the planet was near. Now since Kepler's law says that in equal times it sweeps over equal areas, you will find it must go more slowly when it is far away from the sun than when it is near. This Kepler saw, and so he expressed this law – which he disliked, because it was not harmonious enough for him – he expressed it often or usually, when he referred to it, in the form that the distance of the planet from the sun is inversely related to its velocity. The greater the distance, the smaller the velocity. This is the way in which Kepler referred to the sun, although this particular formulation is mathematically incorrect. The only correct formulation is that in equal times, the radius vector sweeps over equal areas. The other formulation is a very rough approximation, but actually incorrect. Now Kepler *had* the correct formulation, but he disliked it, because it was not simple enough for his harmony idea, and the proportionality was simpler. So, although he had the right law, he very often put it in the wrong form, which was nearer to his intuition of harmony – you probably know that in Greek times, harmony and proportionality were very closely related – so the proportionality law was much more fitting to the harmony of the world which he was looking for. Now this is a very clear indication that he wasn't really aware that this law, and not the harmony law, was solving his problem. Before Newton, we could not see that this law was a very harmonious law – only Newton's wonderfully simple derivation of the law shows really how simply and harmoniously it can be derived. Newton shows that this law is valid for *every* movement in which any force acts upon a body from a certain given centre. It does not matter whether the force is strong or zero; constant or weak or variable. It does not matter whether the force is repulsive or attractive. All that matters is the direction towards the centre. If this is so, the second of Kepler's laws emerges. So it is an extremely general law, and very beautifully derived by Newton. But Kepler did not know the derivation and therefore did not like the law – his own law. Now this shows how the problem situation is, and how we may only afterwards really see what the problem was the scientist solved. But then we can also see what the problem situation was for him, and there is a gap between these two things. How he saw the problem situation is quite different from what the problem situation actually objectively may have been – the problem situation in which he was working. That is a very important distinction.

Your other question about pseudo-problems is a question about different ways of using the term 'problem' – namely, from the point of view of hindsight, and from the point of view of the person or animal which acts under certain pressures. There are all sorts of things to say here. But I wouldn't say that the mere fact that someone hasn't yet come to a problem – that he hasn't yet discovered it – means that it is a pseudo-problem. It may be a very real problem and a very important problem for him, but he hasn't yet discovered it. It may, in fact, take years for someone to recognize and to formulate a problem in a way that he can work on it. He may, in fact, never discover it at all. He may, for example, have vague feelings that something is wrong – with his theory. And he may have these vague feelings for many years. But he may actually never be able to say exactly what it is – or he may never be able to say it in a way that would allow him or others to work on it. Still, the problem may be very important, and it may be not at all anachronistic. It may be a very *timely* problem for him at the time at which he is working on his theory. It may be the problem that he *should* have been working on. But he cannot say what it is. You understand.

There are really all sorts of possibilities here, and it is also connected with the problem of demarcation. So I should really say that I do not use the term 'pseudo-problem' in the same way in which positivist philosophers use it. Carnap, for example, says – it is in his *Scheinprobleme in der Philosophie* – his *Pseudo-problems in Philosophy* – but it is also in his Schilpp volume – Carnap says that metaphysical problems are pseudo-problems, and that the statements of metaphysics are pseudo-statements. This, in fact, was his reason for seeking a criterion of demarcation – to eliminate metaphysics – and it really all goes back to Wittgenstein, who said that the meaning of a sentence is the method of its verification, and who says in his *Tractatus* that science can say all that can be said, and that after that there can be no unanswerable questions left. So these unanswerable questions were called 'pseudo-questions' or 'pseudo-problems', and when Carnap and other positivists said that a problem was a pseudo-problem, they meant that it could not be answered – that it could not be solved – because no possible answer to it could be *verified*.

Now I agree with you that all of this is too simple, and perhaps also too absolute. But I deny all of it, because, first of all, I do *not* agree that the meaning of a sentence is its method of verification, and I do *not* agree that we can, or that we even should try to, eliminate metaphysics. But more important, I deny it because there are many problems which cannot be solved, even in science – and which certainly cannot be solved in the way in which the positivists thought, so that their solutions can be verified – and because these problems do not become pseudo-problems simply because we cannot solve them. A theory is true or false even if we cannot determine its truth or falsity, and a problem may be a real problem even if we cannot solve it. It is all too simple and too convenient to say that a problem is not a problem simply because I cannot solve it. I may never be able to say, even in principle, what would count as a solution to a problem. This may require great genius – just to say what would *count* as a solution, which is, of course, different from actually *giving* a solution. You understand. It may be beyond my abilities. It may be beyond *everyone's* abilities for many years, perhaps even for ever. And yet, the problem would still *have* a solution, even though I would never be able to *say* what it is.

So why, then, distinguish between metaphysical problems and the problems of empirical science? Why do so if not to eliminate metaphysics? And what do *I* mean when I call a problem 'pseudo-scientific'? It happens, sometimes, that someone claims that a problem is a problem for empirical science. But the theory that is proposed to solve the problem actually cannot be tested by *observations*. That is to say, there are really no observations possible that can help us to decide whether this theory is true or false – though the scientist who proposes the theory may in fact think that there are. Freud, for example, claimed that his psychoanalytic theory – which he originally proposed to solve the problem of hysteria – was a theory of empirical science. But it was impossible to test his theory against observations, since it explains a person's behaviour in terms of unconsciously repressed desires – and these are compatible with anything that we can observe. Now many people actually think that this is a strength of Freud's theory – that it is compatible with all possible observations – but I think that it is in fact a great weakness, since it makes it impossible for us to test it and hence to learn from its mistakes. So these are the problems – and the theories – that I call 'pseudo-scientific'. I mean only that the pseudo-scientific theory is said to be empirical, but that it cannot be tested by *observations* – that observations cannot help us to decide whether it is true or false. It is, however, an entirely different thing to say that the theory is *neither true nor false* – for Freud's theory may be true, despite the fact that it cannot be tested – and it is also different to say that the problem cannot be solved.

Of course, I did not propose this distinction between problems that can be tested by observations and problems that cannot be tested by observations in order to eliminate *problems* – and certainly not to suggest that pseudo-scientific theories are meaningless, or that they are neither true nor false. I only wanted to address an important practical problem – namely, the problem of whether or not to test a theory by observation. This can be a very important problem. If nothing else, it can save someone a good deal of time, energy, and, of course, money if he can, in advance, say whether or not his theory can be tested by observations. This may, of course, be very difficult to say, and it is not always possible to say it. But it can be very important.

Someone may, for example, devote many years to searching for observations in order to test a theory that is compatible with every possible observation. And someone may, on the other hand, try to refute a theory without ever thinking to test the theory with the observations that might actually refute it. The most famous example, perhaps, is Hegel. Many of you know that Hegel worked on the problem of the planetary orbits in his dissertation. But Hegel apparently believed that this was a problem to be solved by pure reason, since he attempted to give an *a priori* proof of Kepler's laws. Hegel agreed with Plato about the number of planets, and he actually constructed in his dissertation a 'proof' which said that only seven planets can exist and, in particular, that no planet can lie between Mars and Jupiter. This was a very real problem at the end of the eighteenth century, since there seemed to be a very wide gap – much wider than expected – between Mars and Jupiter. The astronomer Bode had noticed this gap, and many astronomers conjectured that there might be a planet lying somewhere in between. Many astronomers at the time worked on this problem, and they in fact even formed a special organization which they called the 'Celestial Police' in order to search for planets between Mars and Jupiter. So this was not a pseudo-problem. But Hegel was an admirer of Plato, and he apparently tried to refute this conjecture without ever thinking to test his 'proof' against observations. Hegel predicted that there could be no such planet. And this was unfortunate, since there had, by the time he published his prediction, *already* been observed an asteroid – which is, of course, a small planet – between Mars and Jupiter. This asteroid – it is called Ceres – was discovered earlier in the same year that Hegel completed his dissertation, but Hegel did not know about it. Still more asteroids were discovered later – and larger planets like Neptune and Pluto were, of course, discovered later still. But even though Hegel acknowledged his mistake, he still attempted to give an *a priori* account of the planets in his *Encyclopedia*.

This, anyway, is the type of thing that I want to call attention to. Hegel, of course, did not claim that his theory was an empirical theory, and he did not try to test it with observations. That is what he *should* have done. But he did not do it, and this shows the other side of the coin.

4

DESCRIPTION, ARGUMENT, AND IMAGINATION

Ladies and Gentlemen:

Last time I talked mainly about evolution, and I briefly outlined a theory of evolution which may be regarded as a slight revision of neo-Darwinism, or what is nowadays often called 'the new synthesis'.

My theory of evolution is based on my oversimplified tetradic schema,

$$P_1 \to TT \to EE \to P_2$$

Here, TT may be a tentative theory, but it may be, more generally, a tentative trial. EE, as before, is error elimination – not necessarily by way of critical discussion, but also, for example, due to natural selection or, at any rate, due to a failure to solve the problem P_1. P_2 is, of course, the new problem, which may arise either from the error elimination or from the tentative trial.

My main theses were the following six assertions.

1   All living things are engaged constantly in problem-solving, in the sense of this oversimplified tetradic schema.
2   *Individual organisms* solve their problems by tentative trials. These tentative trials consist of *behaviour* patterns.
3   *Species* solve their problems by tentatively composing genetic patterns, including new mutations. These are tried out in the *breeding of individuals*, and this is where natural selection comes in.
4   The tetradic schema explains emergent evolution, that is, the emergence of something entirely novel. Since P_1 and P_2 are only loosely connected, P_2 will often be totally different – even qualitatively different – from P_1. For example, in connection

with the evolution of the species, P_1 may be the problem of increasing fertility: this is one of the most important factors in the survival of the species. Now P_2 may be the new problem of how to avoid being suffocated by one's offspring. (Compare the problem of transport and traffic.)

Or, on the level of the individual organism and its behaviour, P_1 may be due to the slow drying up of large pools containing fish. This may pose for the individual fish a problem of insufficient supply of food within the pool in which the fish finds itself. Then TT may consist in a changed behaviour of this fish. For example, the organism in question may invent a new behavioural *aim*: the aim of getting from one pool to another over dry land. With it, it invents a new problem P_2: *how* to get from one pool to another. P_1 was the problem of how to get food. P_2 is the problem of how to get over dry land. It is clear that these two problems are completely different – qualitatively different.

Thus P_2 may be an entirely new problem – one that has never before arisen (although it may arise in stages) – while P_1 was a very old problem, that of getting enough food.

This shows that our schema can explain the evolutionary emergence of qualitative novelty. For a novel problem may evoke novel responses – that is, entirely new tentative behaviour. Thus emergent evolution, the evolution of *novelty*, is explained by the possible novelty of P_2 as compared with P_1.

5 According to our schema, new behavioural aims, such as getting over land into another pool, will be followed by new *skills* – and these may become *traditional* in a population of fish. If they do, then those anatomic mutations which make it even slightly easier to practise the new skills will be of immediate advantage. They will be favoured by natural selection.

6 Thus, behavioural changes are more important than anatomic changes: anatomic changes cannot succeed unless they favour existing behavioural patterns, and this means successful behavioural patterns. New behaviour is the ultimate spearhead of evolution.

We also see that in the evolution of behaviour, the tentative trying out of new *aims* (a certain type of food) must come before the tentative trial of new *means* (the use of flippers for transport over land), and especially before the trial of new *skills*. Only if new behavioural aims and new skills have been found, and have become traditional, does it become possible for small favourable genetic mutations of the *anatomy* to become sufficiently significant to be of serious advantage, and so to count for natural selection.

Thus we have, as a typical evolutionary sequence: first the aim structure changes, then the skill structure changes. And only then does the anatomic structure change.

But I do not, of course, assert that nothing else *can* happen.

The main problem for today will be to apply evolutionary theory to man. Seen in one way, my lecture today may be said to be on *human nature*, although I personally dislike the use of this vague term.

My first main thesis is that man is distinguished from animals through the peculiarity of human language, and that human language is distinguished from all animal languages in that it serves at least two functions which animal languages do not serve. I will call these functions the 'descriptive' or 'informative' function, and the 'argumentative' or 'critical' function. These are the typical higher functions that are characteristic of man.

My thesis says, further, that these functions constitute human language as the first and basic region of the human world 3.

To put it in another formulation:

3 *products (such as books, stories, myths: language)*
2 *dispositions of the organism*
1 *physical states*

While animal languages do not transcend the region of dispositions – either dispositions to *express* certain emotional states or dispositions to *react* to such expressions – the human languages, which of course are *also* dispositional, transcend the region of dispositions, and so become basic for the third world.

My second main thesis is that the imaginative power of man can, as a result, evolve in entirely new ways. For with the invention of descriptive language, man has the means of saying things which are true, and also things which are not true: he can *invent* stories, fairy-tales, myths. He has thus the means for imaginative invention, and with it he may develop an entirely new kind of imaginative world. True reports may *explain* what has happened: 'The stag died because I hit it with an arrow.' But for the inexplicable, a tale may be invented: 'The king died because Zeus hit him with his thunderbolt.' Thus, explanatory theories may be invented.

This inventive power has its roots in the hereditarily entrenched descriptive function of the human language.

Stories, myths, and explanatory theories are the first characteristic inhabitants of world 3. They are followed by picture stories, such as reports of a hunt, as found in caves. For a long time, pictures are the only means of telling a story other than by way of mouth. Out of this develops picture language and written languages.

In the remaining part of my lecture I will discuss the evolution of the specific human functions of language. I will discuss the whole schema here.

This demands a description of the difference between animal language and human language.

Animal languages, including human languages, may be regarded as kinds of subjective knowledge – that is, as dispositions to behave in a certain way. They may also be regarded as something physical and objective – as exosomatic tools, tools developed outside the body, comparable to nests.

This latter interpretation is obvious in human written, printed or recorded language. But it has forerunners in certain animal languages – for example, in the stumps or trees used by various canine and ursine species as a post office where they deposit their personal scents, and which they use to mark the regions they regard as their private property with signposts that mean: 'Private property. Trespassers will be prosecuted.'

According to students of animal behaviour, the songs of birds have a very similar meaning.

I have mentioned the general idea of exosomatic instruments in my first lecture. This idea is due to Samuel Butler, the author of *Erewhon*, a great admirer and the first great critic of Charles Darwin. Butler noticed that while animals develop new organs, humans develop new tools. As I have said before, instead of growing better eyes and faster legs, we grow spectacles and motor cars.

Now Butler was, of course, quite right to stress that the evolution of exosomatic organs – that is, of tools – is highly characteristic of the human species. But like almost all human peculiarities, this evolution has its animal antecedents. A bird's nest, a spider's web, the dams built by beavers are but three examples of exosomatic instruments evolved by animals. And as we have just seen, even language, and even written language, has such animal antecedents.

These products of animal behaviour – which, of course, all have their genetic basis, even though some have a traditional component

– may be said to constitute the animal antecedent of what has become, on the human level, world 3.

It is important to note that these animal antecedents – these animal third worlds – are, like our own world 3, autonomous. The making of a spider's web or a bird's nest, though instinctive, is in each case adjusted to the objective problem situation created by the animal's instincts in combination with the special environmental conditions which the animal cannot alter. Although the animal can select the least difficult environmental or ecological niche, it is confronted with the unintended consequences of its action once it has selected it.

A simple example is the development of an animal path through the jungle. A path may be described as a tool, but also as a social institution. Where an animal has once broken through the undergrowth, there the path becomes easy and is, according to something like a law of least resistance, therefore used by more and more animals – friends and foes alike – which creates its new and unintended problems.

I now come to my third main thesis. It is this. Although animals have produced their own world 3, consisting of animal languages, no animal has produced anything like objective knowledge. All animal knowledge is dispositional. And though some of these dispositions develop by imitation – that is, by tradition, which admittedly comes near to objective knowledge – there is a gulf between this and human objective knowledge.

Thus, the existence of objective knowledge seems to be one of the few important biological facts which distinguish fairly sharply between animals and men. This suggests that an evolutionary study of the emergence of objective knowledge may be of considerable interest.

My fourth main thesis is this. Though man has evolved most conspicuously through evolving exosomatic tools, it appears that none of these tools – not even the use of sticks – has a specialized hereditary basis, as have apparently all exosomatic tools evolved by animals. This is in itself interesting and surprising. But there is one great exception to this rule: those specifically human functions of language which make objective knowledge possible *do* have a highly specific and specialized and hereditary basis in man, as I shall explain.

My four theses together yield the conjecture that the evolution of man has given man something characteristically and specifically human – a genetically based instinct to acquire, by imitation, a specifically human language which is fit to be the carrier of objective knowledge.

I turn next to the problem of analysing the lower and higher functions of human language. By the lower functions I mean those functions which, based entirely on dispositions, are shared by human and animal languages. And by the higher functions I mean those which are specifically human and which form the basis of world 3.

A theory of these functions was first proposed by Karl Bühler. It is not a fashionable theory. To my knowledge it has been widely ignored by philosophers and psychologists alike, in spite of its great significance.

Bühler distinguished three functions – two lower and a higher one. To this I have added several further higher functions, and especially one which is essential for objective knowledge, and which I will count as the fourth function.

Higher linguistic functions (basis of world 3):	Argumentative or critical function Descriptive or informative function
Lower linguistic functions:	Communicative function Expressive function

Bühler's lower functions of language are the (self-) expressive and communicative functions. His higher function is the descriptive or informative function. The second higher function essential for objective knowledge, a function which I have added to Bühler's schema, is the argumentative or critical function.

The biological and evolutionary character of this schema makes itself felt in that if any of these functions is present, then all of the ones below it are also present. Thus, an animal or a man cannot communicate without expressing its or his inner physiological state. And a man cannot describe something or inform others about something without communicating and without expressing himself.

Similarly, he cannot argue without at the same time activating all the three functions below the argumentative level.

Incidentally, I do not wish to discuss here such other higher functions as the admonitory, the hortative, the incentive, the laudatory, and the derogatory functions. The command function is, essentially, an aspect of the lower functions: 'Do not trespass or else ... !'

Considered biologically, the function of a command, like that of certain drugs, is to *release* certain actions or reactions, or sequences of actions and reactions. Note that the use of signals within a computer can be interpreted as a kind of command language. The same holds for the genetic code. In both cases, *we* may interpret the command so that it also contains a description of what the command is to achieve. But we have every reason to believe that it is not so interpreted within the computer or the cell.

Let me illustrate my schema of the four major functions of language with the help of examples. When a man or a lion yawns, he gives expression to a physiological state of his organism. If a man yawns in his solitary bedroom, his yawn has, *qua* language, no other function than self-expression. If he yawns in company, he may infect others with his state of sleepiness: you can try out yourself how by persistent suggestive yawning – assuming that it is judiciously natural and apparently unconscious – you may not only induce other people to yawn, but you may actually help them to fall asleep. Thus, yawning may have not only an expressive function but also a communicative function of the 'infectious' type. Similarly, the expression of fear tends to induce fear in other individuals. But not all communication is of the 'infectious' type. Expressive acts may, of course, be communicative in a very different way. For example, symptoms of fear may encourage an aggressor, while symptoms of courage may discourage him. And expressions amounting to a command such as 'Keep quiet!' may or may not be of the infectious type of communication, according to whether it is whispered or shouted.

Generally speaking, communication takes place, according to Bühler, whenever an expressive movement in one individual operates upon another as a signal that releases a response in that other individual. Of course, there are also signals which are not expressions. But it is important that most philosophers of language have not got beyond expression and communication, and that few have even distinguished between the two. Everything is called either 'communication' or 'expression' – some stress expression, others communication. Nobody really stresses the other functions.

Let us look now at the third function, the *descriptive function*. While I am speaking to you I am describing to you various things. I am describing Bühler's theory, trying to give you some information about it. And I am also describing various kinds of expressions in men and animals, and the response to them in other men and animals.

But I cannot talk to you, or even prepare my lecture, without expressing some state of my organism.

My voice and my accent, for example, are surely symptomatic of my past history, and therefore expressive. Also, I cannot talk to you without communicating, without, that is, releasing some emotional response in you.

Thus, description normally involves expression and communication. But according to Bühler, this does not make the action of describing a special case of communicating, or communication a special case of expression. This is very important. In fact, the unavoidable self-expression involved in the description may be quite unimportant as compared with the description. And in a good lecture, the response of the audience will be mainly a response to the content of the lecture – to certain world 3 objects – and only in a minor way will it be a response to the lecturer's unavoidable self-expression.

Here, the terms 'descriptive function' and 'informative function' should be taken in a very wide sense. What is intended is a kind of discourse which may be a true or false description of some state of affairs – and the state of affairs may range from such concrete topics as the state of the weather in Atlanta or the state of your health to such very abstract facts as the invalidity of the theorem of Pythagoras in non-Euclidean geometries or the neglect of Bühler's theory among philosophers and psychologists.

But let me now return to Bühler's thesis that it is a mistake to interpret a description as a special case of communication, and communication as a special case of expression. Bühler's point may be put as follows: biologically, the communicative function of language is different from the expressive function – and we may add that, of the two, the communicative function is the more important one from the biological point of view. Similarly, the descriptive function of language is different from the communicative function – and we may add that biologically it is still more important.

It is interesting to note that, although the descriptive function plays its part in full only in human language, near approaches to this function seem to occur in some animal languages. Perhaps the best example is the dance language of the bees. A 'dancing' bee first *expresses* its excitement at having found a promising new place for gathering honey. Second, it *communicates* its excitement to other bees. And third, we may say that it *describes* the direction relative to the position of the sun, and perhaps even the distance from the hive, in which the bees must fly in order to find the new place. In other words, it describes the position in terms of sun-and-hive coordinates.

There is every reason to think, however, that a bee is unable to tell a lie or to tell a story. It *may* make a mistake – in fact, we may induce it to do so by deceiving it – but such mistakes seem to be far too rare to pose a biological problem for the bees, or to make it worth while for them to evolve anything like a method of critically cross-examining an information-carrying bee, or of arguing about its credibility.

To tell a story, to tell lies, seems to have been left to the human animal. But I do not intend to say that man is the only animal that can lie: Ernest Thompson Seton and Konrad Lorenz have both described behaviour in dogs that can well be described as dissimulation – incidentally, the dog described by Lorenz had a charming personality, and was dissimulating only to cover up an embarrassing mistake.

Human language is descriptive in the sense that we can tell a story that is true or false. And this leads to the various logical operations of negation or rejection – that is, to criticism. We can, for example, reject a claim or a suggestion or a piece of information. We can say, 'This piece of information is not true.' Remembering the way in which some higher animals train their young, it is perhaps not too far-fetched to think that our forefathers began this evolution when they told their children, 'Don't do this!' That is to say, negation or rejection may have started with a command such as 'Don't!' Dogs, for example, can learn to understand this quite easily. From this situation, we may have gone on to 'Don't believe it!' (or 'Don't believe him!') The English negation 'No!' can still function in these and other ways.

Of course, things may have evolved very differently. Questions may have played a role, and also children's curiosity, which they share with kittens and other young animals. At any rate, a momentous step was taken when a piece of descriptive information became problematic and was rejected. Only when taking this step, which almost reaches the fourth function, does the descriptive function become fully distinct from the communicative function.

Since the expressive and communicative functions are genetically more deeply rooted than the descriptive function, listening to a story – and, even more, seeing it performed as a play – still has a strong tendency to carry us along emotionally, and to induce some kind of acceptance in us, even if we are fully aware of the fact that the story is only a story. Advertising rests almost completely on this communicating effect, together with communicative infection discussed above.

Even now there are signs that taking this step must have been extremely difficult.

It was not so long ago that to disagree with a man on a question of factual information meant to 'give him the lie', and was equivalent to a challenge to fight. And the earliest method of dealing with contradictory information seems to have been to let the informants fight it out. This explains why it took so long before the factual or objective truth of a piece of information – that is, its correspondence to the facts – was clearly distinguished from the subjective truthfulness of the informant.

The great problem arises as to why the descriptive use of language was, even in its early stages, biologically so important and successful that it became hereditarily entrenched. For there is every reason to believe that it became part of our heredity: the different linguistic development of a child and, say, a chimpanzee or a dog is not merely due to conditioning. The dog may learn to understand some language very well, including its own name and those of some people. But though it may realize the meaning of 'Shall we go for a walk?', there is no reason to think that this meaning is fully descriptive – though it does, of course, release expectations.

The differences between various descriptive grammatical structures – the differences between questions and answers, and many others – must have some kind of innate genetic basis. Of course, they cannot develop without proper stimuli and without opportunities for practice – that is, for learning by trial and error. But there is no imitation without an instinctive and selective drive to imitate – without a dispositional, though unconscious, behavioural *aim*. All this is particularly clear in Helen Keller's development. Of course, no particular human language is hereditary: every language and every grammar is traditional. But the drive, the need, the aim, and the aptitude or skill necessary to acquire a grammar are all hereditary: we inherit merely the potentiality – but this is a good deal.

It is an interesting problem to ask why this specific genetic basis for acquiring a descriptive language evolved. The problem is the more interesting as language seems to be the only one of our exosomatic tools which has a specific genetic basis.

As a tentative solution to this problem, I submit the following tentative list of biologically important effects of the evolution of a descriptive language.

1   A fuller awareness of time and thus a partial replacement of instinctive anticipation by a *more flexible conscious anticipation of future events* – an anticipation that results from plugging into objective knowledge. An example is the knowledge of the changing seasons.

2   The formulation of *questions* and, with it, the beginning of an objectivization of *problems* which were previously merely felt – such as hunger and cold, and how to avoid them.

3   The development of imagination (also to be found in animals!) used in myth-making and story-telling.

4   The development also of inventiveness: the method of trial and the elimination of error presupposes a supply of trials, that is, of new ideas. Imagination vastly increases this supply so that the trial-and-error method may lead to many new kinds of behavioural responses, including the invention and use of tools and social institutions. Language itself is a social institution, and it is the basis of many other social institutions – such as religious, legal, and scientific institutions.

5   The *traditional entrenchment* – rather than the genetic entrenchment – of these newly invented forms of behaviour, tools, and social institutions. These newly invented forms became traditional and remained traditional, owing to a need for flexibility. The same holds for the different human languages.

This tentative list shows some of the biological advantages of a descriptive language. Each of them has its animal predecessors. But the central point seems to be 3: although there is some imaginative inventiveness to be found in higher animals, it obviously increased tremendously with the invention of story-telling. Its role in the rise of the higher civilizations cannot be exaggerated.

Story-telling is found, in so far as we know, in all human communities, however low they may be in their cultural development. Sticks are not found in all human communities, but story-telling is. So I would say that the invention of tools, and the richness of the different tools which men can invent, is connected with story-telling. And those anthropologists who believe that the human hand, which can hold the stick or catch a stone, is the main thing for men – apart, perhaps, from the brain – are, I believe, mistaken. The brain, I think, is all-important. The behaviour and the behavioural function always lead, and this actually has made the flexibility and the incredible richness of human tools possible.

I do not need to say much more about the fourth function of language, the critical and argumentative function. It is obvious that it grows out of, and is closely related to, the descriptive and informative function. There is not very much difference between a child's persistent questions and the persistent cross-questioning of a bearer of suspect information. But while the former may be said to belong to the descriptive function, the latter belongs to the critical function. Almost all conversation and even most stories are largely argumentative and critical. Myths are invented as explanatory theories and are, like all explanations, partly argumentative, although often in a primitive way. It is also obvious that the descriptive function cannot *fully* develop without the critical function: only with the argumentative and critical function can negation and similar things develop, and these, of course, greatly enrich the descriptive and informative function.

From a biological point of view, the fourth function is still very much in the making, and not so well entrenched in our heredity as the others – though the appearance of mathematical child prodigies indicates that there are genetic trials going on in this direction. But there can be no doubt that there is a considerable genetic basis for the critical and argumentative use of human language. Its biological advantages are only too obvious: it is this use which allows us to let theories die in our stead.

I now come to the concluding problem of this lecture: the development of the regulative ideas of objective truth and validity.

The subjective human virtue of truthfulness is a thing which may have been realized even before the evolution of a critical function of language. It assumes, somewhat naively, the identity of a disposition of sincerity with a disposition to say only what is actually the case. And it even involves, though in a confused way, the idea of objective truth: the idea that a story is true if it relates the facts as they are, or as they actually did happen. This is the idea of objective truth, and it is somewhat involved in the idea of subjective truthfulness: the idea that a story-teller is truthful if he relates the facts as they are, or as they actually did happen.

Now the idea of objective truth emerges on the argumentative or critical level, but it does so only in the presence of the descriptive or informative level. Objective truth is the truth of a story or a theory or a report or something like that. All of that occurs on the descriptive level. But the *evaluation* of truth occurs on the argumentative or critical level: we have gone beyond the informative function and the description of events once we begin to evaluate or criticize those descriptions. In this way, the argumentative or critical function of language may be said to emerge from the descriptive or informative function. The argumentative function and the possibility of criticism emerge from the descriptive level with the conscious or unconscious underlying assumption that the story or theory under discussion is to be evaluated from the point of view of its truth.

When I speak of the argumentative or critical function, I am, of course, speaking of criticism always in this sense: from the point of view of truth-finding. I do not, for example, mean 'criticism' in the sense of literary criticism. In literary criticism the term is extended so that you may accept that a story is false and then criticize its literary merits. And there are, in non-literary criticism, other important points besides the truth of a story to be evaluated – such as its relevance or its completeness. These two points presuppose that the story is told in order to solve some *problem*. But even in these cases, criticism will inevitably involve an evaluation of truth. For if we are critical, we will inevitably ask whether or not it is *true* that our story has these literary merits, and whether or not it is *true* that it is relevant or complete. So we can, I think, say quite generally that truth functions as a regulative idea for criticism.

The idea of *validity* – the validity, namely, of an argument or a criticism – also emerges on the argumentative or critical level. And it too functions as a regulative idea, but it pertains to *arguments* and *criticism* rather than to stories or theories. It functions, however, in a manner fully analogous to that in which truth pertains to stories or theories. Just as we may in a critical way try to evaluate a story or theory, so we may in a critical way try to evaluate a critical argument for or against a story or theory.

So we have the following situation. The idea of truth pertains to description and information, but it emerges only in the presence of argument and criticism. This is because to say that a theory is true or false is to pass a critical judgement on it. The idea of validity is then related to the argumentative or critical function in the same way in which the idea of truth is related to the descriptive or informative function: to say that a criticism or an argument is valid or invalid is also to pass a critical judgement on it. But with the idea of validity we have, so to speak, to step higher up in criticism and critically judge our argument or our criticism in order to say whether or not it is valid.

To sum up. The two lower functions of language are much more deeply entrenched in the genetic composition of human heredity than the higher functions. Yet there is little doubt that the descriptive function, and with it the ability to learn grammatical rules in general – though not a *specific* grammar, which is traditional and institutional – and even such traditions as story-telling have a fairly specific genetic basis. And something approaching it may also be said about the argumentative function, though here individual differences seem to be much greater, as the occurrence of mathematical prodigies shows.

This critical or argumentative function has become immensely important since the rise of science in the Ionian School in approximately the time of Thales – something like 500 BC. Since then, objective knowledge has become scientific knowledge.

DISCUSSION

Questioner 1: This is not a substantive question. I just wonder if you have had much feedback – or criticism – from professional anthropologists, linguists, and other such people concerning your conjecture?

Popper: I have had some positive feedback from just, I think, two evolutionary psychologists. One of them is especially interested in animal behaviour and the other is especially interested in the behaviour of certain Africans and in the language development of certain African tribes. He has visited Africa and studied there – especially colour words and such things. This is Professor D.T. Campbell. Apart from him, I have had some other positive feedback from a young animal psychologist who is very excited about these theories. But otherwise, I should say nobody cares. And philosophers who are, incidentally, concerned with language analysis never speak about the function of language, but rather speak about words, and language games, and such things which have really nothing to do with it at all. That is very natural. Why should one expect to have a quick response? Responses always take thirty years, or something like that. There was a time lag of something like seventy or eighty years between John Stuart Mill's formulation that the aim of modern social policy is high wages and short working hours, and the actual coming into practice of this. You find this in John Stuart Mill as a sharp formulation of his social programme, but it has taken a long time to lead to its modern realization. So I don't expect anything like a really positive response in my lifetime. Of course, there are some examples of some quick, positive responses, but they are very rare.

Questioner 2: It seems to me there is a large portion of the field of poetry that would come closest in those four groups to the communicative group. I was wondering if you would consider these poems to be one of the lower functions of language – rather lower functions than higher functions?

Popper: Yes, but of course, very much under the influence of a development of the higher functions. If you go back to the beginning of western poetry – that is to say to Homer – you have, of course, real descriptive poetry. But lyrical poetry, and especially very modern lyrical poetry, is a sort of degenerative decline into completely expressive and communicative levels. And this is not an accident, but is due to mistaken philosophical theories about art. Strangely enough, most philosophers – not all – assert that art is on this level, which is, of course, untrue. It isn't. From Homer on it certainly isn't. And if you look at the cave paintings – which is the oldest art of which we know – then it is story-telling, and certainly comes after the oral story-telling. It is very interesting, and it has been suggested by my friend Ernst Gombrich, that the development from the Egyptian to the Greek art – that is to say, towards a more naturalistic art – is in the main due to Homer, especially to Homer's description of such things as the shield of Achilles. In this description of the shield of Achilles, Homer describes the wonderful work of art in which everything is so very natural. This is the model which the Greek painters then tried to realize. So from the Homeric description, from the word-of-mouth description, from the influence of that word-of-mouth description, then comes Greek painting

– vase painting – which is almost entirely illustrations of Homeric scenes. So you see the influence of Homer on the artist. And it is certainly not too bold a conjecture that the cave paintings were also preceded by word-of-mouth reports about hunts. A cave painting of a hunting scene is an illustration of a story told. Of course, like the story, it has a strong communicative function. That is to say, people should live with the narrator, should experience the excitement of the narrator. Nobody denies that the expressive and communicative function plays a greater role in art than, perhaps, in science. However, to make this the *sole function* of lyric poetry – or of all modern poetry – is really the result of a mistaken philosophical theory. This is the mistaken philosophical theory that art is self-expression and communication – imitative communication, communication on the level of direct response, such as fear – that it is exciting direct response. You understand. This is actually the leading aesthetic theory and, as such, it is very influential, especially on journalists. And from the journalists it goes into art criticism and from art criticism it goes into art.

Questioner 2: The way you are talking down communicative poetry as opposed to descriptive poetry, are you putting a value judgement and saying that descriptive poetry is generally of a higher value than communicative poetry?

Popper: I am sure. There are few works of poetry which are of such high value as Homer's works or, let us say, Shakespeare's works, which are all very largely on the descriptive level. That they are great on the other levels is completely in keeping. Why shouldn't they be? Especially, as I say, an actor has to be very great on the expressive and communicative level.

Questioner 2: Then programme music – would you put that on a higher level than you would put, say... ?

Popper: No. But then, I would deny that what corresponds to this in music is programme music. I would deny that what corresponds to the descriptive level in music is programme music. Music is another affair. It is certainly in some respects related to language. I would say, for example, that what corresponds to descriptive music would be Bach's *St Matthew Passion*, or something like that, which is certainly not what you would call 'programme music', but which is highly descriptive – narrative and descriptive, and everything. I would say, for example, that opera is descriptive. But there is very much music which is not programme music, and which is not merely on the expressive and communicative level – music for which, as it were, what one may call 'the grammar of music' is extremely important, which it isn't on the purely expressive and communicative level.

Questioner 3: Wouldn't this follow from what you were saying earlier, for example, of Homer: that in fact all art involves plugging into world 3 products? And wouldn't it therefore automatically be higher than communicative?

Popper: Of course, I would say that all art belongs to world 3 and, of course, all art understanding is plugging into – and art production presupposes art understanding and, in so far, also plugs into. . . .

Questioner 3: But wouldn't that suggest that there isn't really such a thing as purely expressive art and purely communicative art?

Popper: Yes – or that purely expressive art and purely communicative art are dead ends which lead to the dissolution of the art in question.

Questioner 4: I wonder if you would care to comment on some of the movements of structuralism on philosophers, linguists, and anthropologists, and then relate this to your notion of truth? You seem to speak confidently of an objective notion of truth, of describing things as they are. There have, of course, been a lot of attempts recently to look more to some sort of mental patterning or mental dispositions to structure things.

Popper: About truth: there is a very old idea of truth which goes back at least to Hesiod, and this old idea of truth means that a story is true if it corresponds to the facts. It may be quite interesting to mention that in this old idea of truth the virtue of speaking the truth is somewhat questioned as a virtue. In Hesiod, the Muses tell Hesiod that what we tell you is true – we, the Muses, tell you the truth – although we could tell an untrue story so that everybody would think it was true, even though it was not. That is to say, we are very clever. We can lie in an extremely convincing way. In Homer, this same kind of virtue is attributed to Odysseus. Odysseus is a man who is very good in council and can speak the truth – but if he wants to lie, nobody can really detect his lies very easily. In other words, he is a very good liar. And so are the Muses. If they want to, they can lie very well. Here you see already two different ideas of truth very clearly distinguished – namely, truth in fictional literature and truth in science. When we say of a great novelist that his novels are very much like the truth, then this is almost literally taken from what the Muses say to Hesiod. So truth in the sense of literary criticism is what the Muses tell Hesiod is good lying – undetectable lying. That is what we call in literary criticism 'truth'. The idea of what I call 'objective truth' – that is to say, a statement is true, or a story is true, if it corresponds to the facts – is a very old idea. It is explicitly formulated by Aristotle, and it has since been very much under attack by philosophers – and, since William James, especially by pragmatists.

However, these attacks were ill-founded, and the objective theory of truth has been defended and re-established by the naturalized American philosopher Alfred Tarski, a very great mathematician and a very great logician. He has given a theory of truth which shows that all these attacks on truth – saying that such a thing did not exist – were mistaken. One interesting consequence of Tarski's theory is the following – a very important one. Although there is truth, there is no *criterion* of truth. That is very important, because most philosophers mix up the idea of truth with the idea of a criterion of truth. They think that if there is an idea of truth, there has to be a criterion of truth attached to it. In other words, they are operationalists. There has to be an operation by which we find out whether or not a thing is true. Now it is quite clear that such an operation does not exist. If it did exist, we would all be omniscient. If there were a criterion of truth, then we would have omniscience. Since we are not omniscient, there cannot be a criterion of truth. But Tarski has proved all that with mathematical means, rather than with the theological means with which I have now tried to prove it. In Tarski's proof of the non-existence of the criterion of truth, Gödel's theory plays a very considerable role. So the concept of truth is in order. Actually, Tarski has given a general method of defining concepts of truth for all artificial languages, and he has shown that in ordinary natural language we can apply the concept of truth without fear, if we are a little bit careful. So the attacks against truth are just bad philosophical eye-wash. But they have had a very important marginal influence on this kind of aesthetic quasi-philosophy which thinks that since it has to deal with art it need not really be so very careful or informed in philosophy.

I don't know if this reply is sufficient. What you mean by 'structural' I just don't understand. I think this is just one of those

vague book words which are at present in use. I know what a
structure is, but I don't believe there is anything in this particular
term. If you can explain it to me, I am very ready to listen. And you
are very welcome to explain it.

I've called truth a 'regulative idea', because even though we have
no criterion of truth, we have lots of criteria of falsehood. These
criteria of falsehood are not always applicable, but we can very often
find out whether something is false. This is why our search for truth
is a *critical* search. We know, for example, that a theory must be false
if it is self-contradictory. Actually, self-contradiction is the main
criterion of falsity, because we try always in criticism to find out
whether the thing to be criticized does not conflict with something
else. I mentioned in my lecture the cross-questioning of people who
give a report. I mentioned that bees have not found it worth while
to cross-question a reporting dancing bee. Now, what is the purpose
of cross-questioning? It is to catch the person being cross-
questioned in some sort of contradiction, or in a statement that
contradicts something which we think we know from some other
source. This is the only real purpose of cross-questioning anybody.
So contradiction is really the main thing by which we discover
falsity, and then we know, at least, that the theory is false. Of course,
we also then know that its negation is true. But that usually does not
tell us much, because the negation of a theory with a great
informative content has always a very low informative content. The
greater the informative content of a theory, the lower the informative content of its negation. So we don't get very much truth when
we have refuted a theory, as a rule. But at least we know where the
truth is *not* to be found, and we can go on with our search. So truth
works in the main as a regulative idea in the search for truth, or in
criticism.

Questioner 5: Is it important to say that it's not so much that
objective knowledge is what is important, but rather, as you say,
when we plug into the world of objective knowledge? Isn't it that
inner penetration that is important, rather than the objective world
itself?

Popper: Yes, if you like. You see, what I call 'objective knowledge'
are theories, conjectures, hypotheses, problems, and so on. This
whole field I call 'the province of objective knowledge within world
3'. Objective knowledge need not be true. It's sufficient if it is a
conjecture which has been criticized and has undergone some tests.

That can already be called 'objective knowledge' according to my terminology as I explained it in the first lecture. So I think this amounts to the same as what you wanted to say, doesn't it?

Questioner 5: I suppose so. One other question I want to ask was the problem that you very nicely explained: how all of the lower levels come under the third and fourth levels. That is to say, the expressive and communicative arts are somehow subjective areas of knowing that animals can take part in. I suppose that I am still getting at – isn't it true that even the third and fourth are still subjective in that sense?

Popper: All language has a subjective component, and in that sense even the third or fourth cannot be without a subjective component. But it is the objective component which we have isolated in the third and fourth. That is the whole point – that it all goes together in practice, all four levels. You cannot, without giving vent to your feelings, speak. You cannot communicate without arousing feelings in other people. Therefore, you cannot describe without expressing yourself and arousing feelings. But that doesn't make the description *as such* subjective. The description is objective in the following very precise sense: namely, it can be criticized from the point of view of objective truth. And the result of the criticism, at least ideally, ought to be completely independent of the first and second levels. Of course it isn't always so, but it can very often be so in very many cases. A scientific discussion may get very heated and lots of emotions may come in. But, by and large, in the course of time, in the course of centuries, the result of scientific discussion is pretty independent of the heat and of the emotional levels which were once attached to it. Who thinks today that Newton's theory aroused nationalist feelings in France? No doubt it did – very much so. You see, the French were for Cartesian physics rather than for New-tonian physics. And Newton's physics actually was explicitly a criticism of Cartesian physics. So there was a rejection of Newtonian physics on nationalistic grounds in France until Voltaire tried to popularize Newtonian physics in a book, which was burned. So who knows today about these things? They are all forgotten, and the objective results still survive. Nobody is particularly heated in discussing Newtonian theory any longer. As long as I speak to you, I cannot repress my emotional and communicative feelings. But in time they will all be forgotten and the theory will be tested.

Questioner 6: Let me see if I get this right. The first three functions of language can be subjective – that is expressive, communicative, and descriptive – and it's only when you bring in a fourth element – argumentative and critical – that you can achieve a different kind of knowledge, that is objective knowledge....

Popper: Which may be on the descriptive level....

Questioner 6: That is, two people come together with their subjective description of an act, and then come together, have a criticism, and then a new kind of knowledge – objective knowledge – can come from this interaction?

Popper: I quite agree. The objectivity of the third level is only achieved when the fourth level comes into action. One can put it in that way. That is the difference – one might subdivide the third level into two levels, namely the 'not yet objectivized descriptive' and the 'objectivized descriptive', and one might say that the bees have actually achieved the not yet objectivized descriptive, even though what they say is always true, or practically always true, unless they are deceived. But that is because their instinct trains them to tell the truth, and also because their language is so poor. For all we know it is actually part of their hereditary make-up, and it is very poor. But you are quite right, I think, that we might subdivide the third level – the descriptive level – into two parts, namely the one on which we achieve objectivity, and the one on which objectivity is not yet achieved. Actually, what Bühler had in mind was achieved objectivity, and this is why I think that his theory goes so far beyond almost all theories of language in which these levels are not explicitly mentioned. I just want to give one example. Most of you who have done any philosophy will know the name of Stevenson, a philosopher of ethics. Stevenson's peculiar contribution to ethics is that he has discovered that ethics is emotive and communicative in my sense. He calls it 'the emotive theory of ethics'. What he means is emotive and communicative – that when we say something is good, then we mean 'you are a good boy', expressing some judgement. Possibly, he says, we try to make him repeat that kind of thing – which would be communicative, but he calls it the expressive theory of ethics. As you see, the basis of Stevenson's expressive theory of ethics is a purely expressive theory of language, and that's really all practically. It may be very well – all he says may be true, but it isn't *all* that is true. There is no doubt that ethics is expressive, and also no doubt that it is also communicative. But has it not also higher functions? *That* is the question. It is an open question which I do not want to discuss now. But what I want to discuss is the *primitivity* of the argument. It does not really ask the question in full. Namely, 'Has ethics no other function *but* expressive and communicative functions?' This would amount to asking, 'Is ethics nothing but animal communications?' This is really what people mean. Is ethics practically on *that* kind of animal level, on the level of 'Don't!'? And is there nothing in addition to 'Don't!' in it? I mean that which the dog understands, because the dog does learn to understand 'Don't!'

Questioner 7: On the same point as before, on the notion and the discussion of the correspondence theory of truth. We have been talking, at least – perhaps not yourself – but people have been talking of *facts*. And when we know facts, do we know propositions, or do we know things? Is this at all important for your description of objective reality?

Popper: I would say theories.

Questioner 7: Well, what is the relation of a theory to the phenomena we see all around us?

Popper: A theory tries to describe phenomena as they are. A theory is a conjecture about not only phenomena, but about the world. Not only phenomena – it describes not only phenomena, where 'phenomena' means just what appears in the world. It does more. A theory, for example, may not only *describe* the phenomenon of this bluish seat here, but may try to *explain* it by something like a chemical or optical theory of paints and dyes. So it is not only about phenomena, but it's a theory that is, as a rule, explanatory, and, so goes beyond phenomena.

Questioner 7: It is possible to construe these explanations or these theories – I mean scientific theories – as symbolic modes of representation and therefore to represent verbally our description of the chemical properties – or anything you want – of a chair. But the point is that there is a whole verbal nexus in the air. What is the relation between that verbal nexus and the physical reality of that chair? It seems to me that there is a certain discrepancy between our language, which is, after all, incomplete – you know – it's not a *perfect* symbolic tool, an exosomatic tool, or whatever you want to call it. What is the relation between this symbolic description and the physical reality?

Popper: Our language is far from being perfect, but it is astonishingly good. Astonishingly powerful. Its drawbacks are constantly dealt with by mathematicians who invent finer and finer tools, finer and finer exosomatic tools. And it is perfectly true that our language will always be incomplete, and that our description of reality will always be incomplete. There is something like an essential incompleteness of all languages, which is connected again with Gödel's theorem. But in spite of this essential incompleteness – after all, who expects that he will ever get complete knowledge? – in spite of the essential incompleteness, it develops more and more, and is so extremely good at describing reality that there is really very little to be complained of and very much to be wondered at and admired, especially very much to be amazed at that human beings have actually produced this incredibly powerful tool. The power of it is, of course, seen in our moonships and atom bombs. But there are many other things. Unfortunately, it is not yet sufficiently powerful to avoid misuse by journalists. But I don't think there is much to be complained about. I don't think anybody will ever say that language is sufficient to penetrate all reality. But it can penetrate beyond any given depth into reality. It can penetrate deeper and deeper. And the correspondence theory – this very interesting thing – how can we really understand the correspondence between language and a fact? This has been dealt with by Tarski and has been very neatly cleared up. However, I am afraid it is almost hopeless to explain here and now Tarski's correspondence theory. In a sense it is very trivial, and in a sense it does really need the realization of one fundamental idea – namely, the idea of a metalanguage, of speaking *about* language. All right. I'll try.

The first step in Tarski's theory is that he speaks about the truth of *statements* – that is to say, of linguistic entities. Now, if we speak about the truth of linguistic entities, we have to speak *about* linguistic entities. In any theory of this kind – any theory like Tarski's – we have to speak about linguistic objects as if they were tables or chairs. That's one thing which has to be clearly understood. A language in which we speak about linguistic objects is called a 'metalanguage'. So any theory of truth must be a metalinguistic theory, because it speaks about properties of a language – the properties of statements, of linguistic objects. Statements are like chairs and tables. Language is like a furniture factory. In saying that a statement is true we say something similar to saying that a chair is comfortable. And in saying *that*, we have to speak in a metalanguage, which is the first thing to be understood. We have to speak *about* a language, and to do that, we have to speak *in* a metalanguage. Now, this language about which we speak is called the 'object language' – the language in which we speak is called the 'metalanguage'. So we have to distinguish, when we develop a theory of truth, between the language in which we speak and the language about which we speak – or between the *metalanguage*, which is the language in which we speak, and the *object language*, which is the language about which we speak. That is the main point in Tarski's theory – this sharp distinction between metalanguage and object language, or the language in which we speak and the language about which we speak.

Once this is made clear, very much is gained. We can now proceed as follows. We can say that most people will agree to start with truth as a correspondence with the facts. Their problem will be how we can speak about correspondence with the facts, or what correspondence with the facts really consists of. How can a statement correspond to facts? It looks very hopeless at first sight. Now there have been many theories about that. One theory is Schlick's theory. He said correspondence with the facts consists of what a mathematician would call a 'one-to-one correspondence'. I don't know whether all of you know what a one-to-one correspondence is, but mathematics distinguishes between many-to-one, one-to-many, and one-to-one correspondences. For example, one can depict a one-to-one correspondence – here are certain objects and there are certain objects, and a one-to-one correspondence is: to every object of this kind belongs an object of that kind. One thing is clear – namely, that truth in language is *not* a one-to-one correspondence. To one fact may correspond many true descriptions. Many different statements or assertions may equally truly describe one and the same fact. For example, if the description 'Peter is taller than Paul' is true, then the description 'Paul is shorter than Peter' is true. There you have at once a proof that truth cannot be a one-to-one correspondence. So Schlick goes out. Then came Wittgenstein. He said truth is a picture. A statement is true if it is a true picture of the facts. It is a picture theory of language. But two things are quite clear – namely, that a statement is only in a metaphorical sense a picture, and that therefore this theory is no good at all. A statement is certainly not a picture in the sense in which a photograph, for example, is a picture. A photograph may be a true photograph – actually, all photographs, unless they are spoilt or falsified afterwards, are true photographs – but a statement is not a photograph and has no similarity to a photograph. So Wittgenstein's theory is only metaphorical, and therefore does not help.

Now comes Tarski's theory of correspondence. This theory is, as it ought to be, trivial. It is *so* simple and *so* trivial that one cannot believe that it solves the problem. And *that* is one of its difficulties. People think it is impossible that this theory should solve the problem – to which one has to answer that if a judge tells a witness to speak the truth, and nothing but the truth, he thinks that the witness knows very well what he says, and that therefore truth *ought* to be something trivial. Now, Tarski's theory is trivial, and at the same time highly sophisticated. The sophistication, however, lies *only* and *exclusively* in the distinction between an object language and a metalanguage. That is its sophistication. Once you have understood this, the theory is completely trivial. Tarski says the following: truth is correspondence to the facts; but if you wish to explain correspondence to the facts, you have to speak in a language in which you can speak about (a) linguistic entities such as statements, and (b) facts. Only in a language in which you can speak about *both* statements and facts can you hope to explain correspondence to the facts. So I have to use language, and the language I have to use has to be rich enough to speak about statements and about corresponding facts. Otherwise, I cannot hope to explain correspondence to the facts. My language has therefore to be a metalanguage, because it speaks about statements. But it has to be more than *just* a metalanguage. It must also be able to speak about facts. Such a language Tarski calls a 'semantic metalanguage'. I don't know whether the term is very fortunate, because the word 'semantic' is one of those dangerous book words in philosophy. Anyway, that is another point. Take it simply as a label: a semantic language is a language with which I can speak about other languages and about facts. *That* is the decisive thing. And especially, I must be able – whenever I am speaking about a statement, I also must be able – to speak about the fact which this statement describes.

We are practically at an end of all the sophistication, and now comes the triviality. This was sophisticated, but everything beyond this is trivial. Tarski says very simply: the statement, quote – now I am speaking about the statement – 'Snow is white' unquote corresponds to the facts if, and only if, snow is white. Now, the only important thing here is this: the statement 'Snow is white' – here I am speaking about the statement – corresponds to the facts if, and only if, snow is white – here I am speaking about the facts. Here in quotes I have a semantic metalanguage – a language in which I can speak about statements by using quotes – and here without quotes a language in which I speak about facts, as in all languages, without using quotes. The normal way in any language to speak about facts is not to use quotes. The most convenient way to speak about statements is to use quotes. So we have the statement 'Snow is white', or, if you like, the statement 'Snow is green' – it makes no difference whatsoever. The statement 'Snow is green' corresponds to the facts if, and only if, snow is green. This explains corresponding to the facts quite generally. It does not make the slightest difference whether I say snow is green or snow is white, because the statement 'Snow is green' corresponds to the facts if, and only if, snow is green. The statement 'Snow is white' corresponds to the facts if, and only if, snow is white – or generally: the statement 'x' corresponds to the facts if, and only if, y, provided 'x' is the *name* of a statement describing y.

Now there is nothing easier than that. So we have established what 'corresponds to the facts' means, quite generally. We have *established* it; this is not a *definition*. Tarski has shown, then, that we can give a definition of 'correspondence to the facts' for any given artificial language. Anyway, that is not really important. But this certainly establishes very fully – although with the use of examples (but since the example can be varied in any way you like, there is no limit to the variation of the examples) – this establishes very fully what 'correspondence to the facts' means. And so it establishes very fully what 'truth' means.

So this, I think, is the relationship between what you have called the 'symbolic description' and the 'physical reality': the symbolic description – that is, the statement – either corresponds to the facts of the physical reality, or it does not. It is, in other words, either true or false. That is the relationship.

5

INTERACTION AND CONSCIOUSNESS

Ladies and Gentlemen:

I hope that you have not forgotten that the main topic of my lectures is the body–mind problem, and that world 3, emergent evolution, and the theory of the evolution of language are to serve as our principal means of proceeding towards a tentative solution of the body–mind problem. In today's lecture I intend to outline a solution of this problem.

I have to warn you, however, that the tentative theory which I intend to propose to you is not only tentative but also not very much of a theory as compared, say, with a theory in the field of physics. It is, however, a testable theory, and it has passed some tests in a way which has exceeded all my expectations.

To those of you who know something of the history of philosophy, I hardly need to say how very unsatisfactory is everything that has been said about our problem so far. It is only in comparison with certain earlier attempts that I think that I have something to offer.

It is interesting to note that our knowledge about our minds, including our own mind, is extremely vague. Our knowledge about our physical behaviour is much clearer. And this, of course, is the reason why it has been studied much more closely.

The term 'behaviourism' is, like most such terms, ambiguous. It may either mean the decision to concentrate upon behaviour and not to worry about states of consciousness, or it may mean, more radically, the denial of the existence of states of consciousness themselves. This more radical theory is also called 'physicalism' – an older term is 'materialism' – and it is very convenient, because, if we adopt it, a great many difficult problems disappear. Its only drawback is that it is false. States of consciousness certainly exist, even though they are vague and difficult to describe, and even though their existence creates difficult problems.

I think that it is necessary, in this connection, to make it quite clear that there are a number of sweeping philosophical theories which are similar to physicalism or materialism or radical behaviourism in their general structure and status – that is to say, theories that are *false*, even though they are *irrefutable*. It is, I think, necessary to discuss this situation here before I proceed any further, because many people think, mistakenly, that a theory which is irrefutable must be true.

One of these irrefutable theories is known by the name 'solipsism'. Solipsism is the theory that I, and only I, exist. According to this theory, the rest of the world – including all of you, and also my body – is my dream. Thus, you do not exist. You are only my dream. This theory cannot be refuted by you. You may assure me of your existence. You may shout, and perhaps hit me, to prove that you exist. All this, of course, can never refute solipsism. For obviously, I can always say that I am dreaming that you are shouting and hitting me. And it is clear that nothing whatever can ever happen that could refute my solipsistic conviction – if I had such a conviction. Of course, I do not hold any view like this. But if any of you chooses to become a solipsist, it will be impossible for me to refute you.

Why am I not a solipsist? Although solipsism is irrefutable, it is a false theory and, in my opinion, it is a silly theory. One *cannot* refute it, but one *can* produce very good, though quite inconclusive, arguments against it.

One such argument is a story which Bertrand Russell tells in one of his books. (I think it is in the Russell volume of Schilpp's Library of Living Philosophers.) Russell reports that he received a letter from a lady who tells him that she is a convinced solipsist and that she has written a book which contains a conclusive proof of solipsism. She indignantly complains that all the publishers to whom she has sent her manuscript have rejected it, and she then asks Russell to intervene on her behalf.

The joke of the story is, of course, that a solipsist should not complain about publishers, since publishers do not exist. Nor should a solipsist ask a non-existing philosopher to intervene on his or her behalf. But this does not, of course, *refute* solipsism. For the lady in question could always answer that it was all part of her dream: that it was her wish dream to see her book published – or, more precisely, to *dream* that her book was published – and that it was her anxiety dream that she would never dream that her book was published.

A similarly inconclusive argument against solipsism – but one which is good enough for me – would be this. When reading Shakespeare, or hearing any of the great composers, or seeing a work of Michelangelo, I am very conscious of the fact that those works go very, very far beyond anything I could ever produce. But according to the theory of solipsism, *only I exist* – so that in dreaming these works I am, in fact, their creator. This is utterly unacceptable to me. And so, I conclude, other minds must exist, and solipsism must be false. Obviously this argument is inconclusive. But, as I said before, it is good enough for me. In fact, in order to believe seriously in solipsism, one would have to be a megalomaniac. An inconclusive argument of this kind is called an *ad hominem* argument. That is not a conclusive argument, but, as it were, an appeal from man to man.

A theory which in content is very different from solipsism, but very similar in its logical structure, occurs in a short story by the philosopher Joseph Popper-Lynkeus of Vienna. It is the story of a young Athenian, nicknamed by his friends 'Little Socrates', who, like Socrates, walks about in Athens challenging people to debate with him. The thesis which he asks others to disprove is that he, Little Socrates, is immortal. 'Try to refute me,' he says. 'You might think you can do it by killing me. But even if I accept provisionally your hypothesis that you can refute me in this way, then, on your own hypothesis, your refutation will come too late for refuting *me*.'

This argument was known in Vienna, where Popper-Lynkeus was widely read. Wittgenstein was so impressed by the irrefutability of the argument of Little Socrates that he accepted it, saying in his *Tractatus* not only that 'death is not an event of life' but also 'he who lives in the present lives for ever'. As opposed to Wittgenstein, I think that, though we are all living in the present, we shall not go on living for ever. And, generally speaking, I am not greatly impressed by irrefutability.

Another version of solipsism is the philosophy of Bishop Berkeley. Berkeley is too modest a man and too good a Britisher to be a solipsist: he recognizes that other minds have a right to exist equal to his own. But he insists that only *minds* exist, and that the existence of bodies and of a material world is a kind of dream which is, due to God's intervention, dreamt by all minds in unison. In other words, the world does not exist except in our minds, that is, in our experience of perceiving the world. Or in still other words, the physical world is *our* dream, just as in solipsism it is *my* dream. But although Berkeley's theory is not megalomaniac, the Bishop should have been shaken by another *ad hominem* argument: his theory is incompatible with Christianity. For Christianity teaches that we are not pure minds or spirits, but embodied minds. And it teaches the reality of bodily suffering.

All these theories are irrefutable, and this fact seems to have greatly impressed some philosophers – for instance, Wittgenstein. But theories asserting the precise opposite are just as irrefutable – a fact that should make us suspicious. As I have often put it, it is a mistake to think that irrefutability is a virtue in a theory. Irrefutability is not a virtue but a vice. I still think that this is quite a good way of putting the matter. But since a somewhat pedantic former student of mine has criticized my formulation, I am now unfortunately forced to explain at length what I mean by it. I mean, of course, that the fact that a theory is irrefutable should not impress us favourably, but should make us suspicious of the theory.

It is clear that both solipsism and Berkeley's theory – called 'idealism' – solve the body–mind problem, because both say that there are no bodies. Now materialism or physicalism or radical behaviourism also solve the body–mind problem. But they do it by the opposite stratagem. They say that there is no mind, that there are neither mental states nor states of consciousness. And they say that there is no intelligence, that there are only bodies which behave as if they were intelligent – by making, for example, more or less intelligent verbal utterances or, more precisely, verbal noises.

This theory is, again, irrefutable. But there is, again, an *ad hominem* argument against it. It is this. We can ask the physicalist: 'To whom do you address your theory? To my body? Or to my more or less intelligent behaviour? Is it your purpose to elicit a verbal utterance from me? It cannot possibly be your purpose to convince me. It can, at best, be your purpose to make my body utter the more or less intelligent verbal noises: "I am convinced." But why all this fuss about verbal behaviour? Or *is* there something like truth and falsity? Yet if all talk about truth and falsity is merely verbal behaviour and nothing else, why should verbal behaviour be worth the trouble of all these endless arguments?'

I do not suggest that these comments can refute physicalism. I personally can only say that I am not sufficiently interested in the verbal noises of physicalists to continue any further with that verbal behaviour of mine which we old-fashioned non-physicalists might describe as an *ad hominem* criticism of physicalism.

Since I have said so much about physicalism, I may just as well say a word about computers: about the claim that our brains, or perhaps our minds, are computers, or vice versa; and about the remark, made with a very serious face, that computers have brains as good as or even better than our own.

Einstein once said: 'My pencil is cleverer than I.' What he meant, of course, was that he could, by using his pencil, get results which he had not foreseen. Quite right: this is precisely the reason why we make pencils and use them. If we could not get further with a pencil than without it, we should not use it.

The same of course holds for computers. A computer is nothing but a glorified pencil: a bigger and better and more powerful and, most important, incredibly expensive pencil. Obviously we should not make these incredibly expensive super-pencils were they not more clever than the ordinary ones.

Physicalism, in brief, denies the obvious – that is, the existence of mental states, or consciousness. Among those which do not deny the obvious existence of mental states, several theories of the mind have been competing for acceptance. There is, first, Descartes' theory. In a slightly modernized form which avoids talking of 'substance', Descartes' theory asserts that mental states and physical states *interact*. His theory is therefore described as 'interactionism'. Since physical states are *located* in space and time, the question arises at which *place* the interaction takes place. Descartes' answer was: 'In the brain, in the so-called "pineal" gland.' This answer of Descartes has been much ridiculed. But I will here propose a very similar answer.

An alternative to interactionism is the theory that physical states and mental states do not interact but run parallel. This theory is called 'body–mind parallelism'. In its simplest and most famous form, due to Spinoza, it says that mind and matter are two aspects of the same thing. If we look at a piece of eggshell from inside, it is concave. If we look at the same piece from outside, it is convex. But the convexity and the concavity are aspects of the same thing. Spinoza suggested that if we look at reality from inside, it is mind, and if we look at reality from outside, it is matter.

This is an ingenious theory, and it may possibly be true. It may be that an electron is invested with consciousness. But according to quantum physics, all electrons are exactly alike, *whatever their history may have been*. In other words, they must be unaffected by their history. Assuming parallelism, this means that, even if they have consciousness, they can have no *memory* whatever. Now consciousness without any memory would consist of flashes of consciousness, each lasting for a minimum length of time and each being completely unconnected with any other. Such a form of consciousness is feasible. But it would be totally different from what we call 'consciousness'. For this depends, entirely, on the connectedness of states of consciousness through some not too short periods of time.

For reasons such as these, I do not think that parallelism can be taken seriously. But there is a theory which may be regarded as a variant of parallelism, and which is more serious. It bears the ugly name 'epiphenomenalism', and it may be described as follows.

Owing to friction, every clock will produce some heat. But this is a by-product which has little or nothing to do with its working: we may understand its mechanism without paying any attention to the small amount of heat produced. An irrelevant phenomenon such as the heat produced by a clock is called an 'epiphenomenon'. In connection with the body–mind problem, epiphenomenalism is the theory that minds do exist, but as epiphenomena – that is, physicalism or materialism or behaviourism are wrong when they deny the existence of consciousness, but they are right in ignoring it. For if mind is an epiphenomenon, then everything of any significance can be put in behaviouristic terms.

Epiphenomenalism shares with parallelism the conviction that the world of physics is complete – or, in other words, that in principle *everything* that can be explained at all can be explained in purely physical terms.

It is this view of the completeness of the physical world which I try to combat by my theory of world 3.

World 3: theories, objective problems
World 2: dispositions to behave
World 1: physical states

The fact that there are objective problems, such as the problems of prime number theory, existing in world 3, together with the fact that the discovery of such a problem may lead to great and obvious changes in world 1, show, I believe, that world 1 is not closed or complete, but open towards world 3, with world 2 acting as intermediary.

If this is so, then epiphenomenalism must be mistaken: mind or consciousness cannot be an insignificant epiphenomenon.

My rejection of epiphenomenalism is also supported by the evolutionary approach: if mind or consciousness is an epiphenomenon, why should it have evolved? Why should it have become more and more prominent with higher animals?

These questions, in their turn, suggest that in order to understand mind or consciousness, and its relation to the physiology of the organism, one should adopt a biological point of view and ask: what is the biological significance of mind? What does mind do for the organism?

All these questions have led me to what I may perhaps call a new theory of the mind and of the ego.

I will begin with the remark that the world of consciousness is as little homogeneous as world 1 or world 3.

There is the difference in kind known to us all between states of consciousness while we are awake and states of consciousness while we are asleep and dreaming. And there are similar differences between a vivid and well-remembered dream and one of which we have only the dimmest memory.

Of animal consciousness we know, of course, very little. But the behaviour of dogs while awake and asleep – either apparently disturbed by dreams or else in a deep sleep – is sufficiently similar to our own behaviour for conjecturing that dogs and other higher animals also have conscious states of various levels.

My first and basic conjecture may, then, be formulated as follows. To speak of body and mind is somewhat misleading, for there are many different kinds and levels of consciousness in the animal kingdom. Many of the lower levels can sometimes be found in our own experience – in dreams, for example, or during hypnosis.

My second conjecture is this. We can distinguish between full consciousness – that is, the highest form of human consciousness – and lower forms, which may be vastly different.

Now the question arises of the biological significance of these various levels of consciousness. This is a question which is difficult to answer. Everything, moreover, is speculative here – even the existence of a lower, or animal, form of consciousness. After all, we can always deny the existence of consciousness altogether, as radical behaviourists or physicalists do. Thus, no cogent arguments in favour of our speculations can be expected to be forthcoming in this field.

But theories are always conjectural, and at least some of my conjectures have testable consequences.

In order to answer the question of the biological significance of consciousness conjecturally, I will introduce two ideas: the idea of a *hierarchy of controls*, and the idea of *plastic control*.

In all higher organisms we find a hierarchy of controls. There are controls regulating the heartbeat, the breathing, and the balance of the organism. There are chemical controls and nervous controls. There are controls of healing processes and controls of growth. And in all freely moving animals, there is the central control of the movements of the animal. This control, it appears, is the highest in the hierarchy. I conjecture that mental states are connected with this central and highest control system, and that they help to make this system more plastic. A control like that which makes us blink when something suddenly approaches our eyes I call a 'non-plastic control'. When the possible reactions cover a wide spectrum of possibilities, I speak of a 'plastic control'.

My next conjecture is this. In all moving animals, there are elaborate warning systems such as eyes or tentacles. There is also an inborn drive to move – that is, to explore the environment, especially in the search for food. The warning system is very specialized. It gives warning of dangers, such as the danger of running into a tree and the danger of an approaching enemy. It also may give a warning of an approaching opportunity, such as an object which may be used for food. Let us call the dangers and the dangerous objects 'biologically negative', and the opportunities 'biologically positive'. The organs of most animals are so built as to distinguish between these classes. That is to say, they *interpret* or *decode* the stimuli that they meet. But this system of interpretation or decoding – which is anatomically, and thus genetically, based – is at first rigid rather than plastic, and does not make allowance for unusual situations, as the example of insects flying against the glass of a windowpane shows. My conjecture is that, by emergent evolution, first vague feelings emerge that reflect the expectation of the animal of negative or positive events, or of incipient withdrawal and advance, and that, by further steps in emergent evolution, these become feelings of pain and of pleasure. These are, in the main, of an anticipatory character. In their turn, they become the basis of a further, or higher level, system of interpretation or decoding of signals which reach the animal – that is, of a system of interpretation or decoding beyond that system which the sense organs themselves provide. Thus, the second world may emerge from the first, and we have already seen how the third may emerge from the second.

In unusual situations, the animal will often misinterpret or wrongly decode the signals it receives. This, I conjecture, leads to tentative interpretations – to a wavering, say, between withdrawal and advance, or between feelings of fear and of courage. And from these may evolve *anticipatory and tentative interpretations of a situation*. They are anticipatory in the sense that they are connected with the incipient innervation of movements rather than with actual movements. This would be a decisive step. The step would mean the tentative trying out of possible movements or of possible reactions, without at once carrying out the actual movements themselves.

The biological advantage of a process of this kind seems clear, and may lead to a stage where various possible lines of behaviour, and their fittingness to the situation, may be tried out, up to a point, without undergoing the risk of making the actual movements.

But this would have to involve a kind of *imagination*: the imagined anticipation of the expected result of the movements – together with a shrinking back from imagined and anticipated results which are biologically negative, and an acceptance of those which are biologically positive – and a consequent action. This, then, is the way in which consciousness interacts with the body. It may be conjectured that this anticipatory trying out is connected with incipient tentative movements or incipient innervations of the organs of motion. Just as the interpretation or decoding of signals may be closely connected with the general state of the organism – that is, with its anticipation of reactions or its readiness to react – so these innervations, which may almost lead to movements, may induce changing and tentative interpretations of the signals received. Thus, an animal in a hungry and aggressive mood will interpret its whole environment differently from, say, a satiated or frightened or wounded animal: the former interprets its environment from the point of view of possible food supply, the latter from the point of view of ways of escape.

Consciousness, on this level, may be connected with interpretation and action embedded in general feelings of pleasure and pain, of activity, curiosity, enterprise, and withdrawal or flight.

It is understandable that this gives the organism a broadening of its central control system by better, as well as more tentative, anticipations of the development of both the environmental situation and its own behavioural reactions.

What I have sketched so far is a kind of general evolutionary background for my new conjectural theory of the human mind and of the human ego. But before proceeding to this theory, let me point out that the relation between mental states and physical states is, according to this theory, fundamentally the same as that between controlling systems and controlled systems – especially with feedback from the controlled to the controlling system. That is to say, it is an *interaction*.

I now come to human consciousness. It contains a great many residues of lower forms of consciousness, such as all kinds of vague feelings mingled with more pronounced feelings of pain. In fact, a human being can, for example, feel a sharp pain, be apprehensive, and be very happy – all at the same time.

Thus, human consciousness is a highly complex affair. The famous idea of a stream of consciousness is all too simple. There are all kinds of levels of consciousness – higher and lower, and the lower ones merging unnoticeably into subconscious or unconscious states. On the other hand, the idea of a stream is influenced by the theory of time – the theory, that is, that time flows.

But there is no doubt that we achieve full consciousness – or the highest state of consciousness – when we are thinking, especially when we try to formulate our thoughts in the form of statements and arguments. Whether we do this silently by speaking to ourselves – as we all do, sometimes, in spite of the fact that this has been denied – or whether we discuss some interesting problem with our friends, or whether we put our theories on paper, there can be little doubt that thinking and arguing happen on the highest level of consciousness. In thinking articulately, we really *know* that we are conscious.

I now come to the formulation of my theory of full consciousness and of the ego or the self. I have five main theses.

1   Full consciousness is anchored in world 3 – that is, it is closely linked with the world of human language and of theories. It consists mainly of thought processes. But there are no thought processes without thought contents, and thought contents belong to world 3.

2   The self, or the ego, is impossible without the intuitive understanding of certain world 3 theories and, indeed, without intuitively taking these theories for granted. The theories in question are theories about space and time, about physical bodies in general, about people and their bodies, about our own particular bodies as extending in space and time, and about

certain regularities of being awake and being asleep. Or to put it in another way, the self, or the ego, is the result of achieving a view of ourselves from outside, and thus of placing ourselves into an objective structure. Such a view is possible only with the help of a descriptive language.

3   Descartes' problem of the location of full consciousness or the thinking self is far from nonsensical. My conjecture is that the interaction of the self with the brain is located in the speech centre. I shall mention in my next and last lecture some experimental tests of this conjecture.

4   The self, or full consciousness, is exercising a plastic control over some of our movements which, if so controlled, are human actions. Many expressive movements are not consciously controlled, and so are many movements which have been so well learned as to have sunk into the level of unconscious control.

5   In the hierarchy of controls, the self is not the highest control centre, since it is, in its turn, plastically controlled by world 3 theories. But this control is, like all plastic controls, of the give-and-take, or feedback, type. That is, we can – and we do – change the controlling world 3 theories.

I will now briefly look back upon the old body–mind problem – that is, upon the question whether there is an *interaction* between body and mind or a *parallelism*. The answer is given by emergent evolution. The novel structures which emerge always interact with the basic structure of physical states from which they emerge. The controlling system interacts with the controlled system. Mental states interact with physiological states. And world 3 interacts with world 2, and through it with world 1.

In my concluding lecture next week I shall speak of the self, rationality, and freedom.

DISCUSSION

Questioner 1: You have five hypotheses, and I am afraid I missed the fourth one and the first.

Popper: The first is that full consciousness is anchored in world 3. That is, it is closely linked with the world of human language and of theories. Full consciousness consists mainly of thought processes. But there are no thought processes without thought contents, and thought contents belong to world 3. So it is a thesis with an argument for the thesis. And the thesis is that full consciousness is anchored in world 3. 'Anchored' is, of course, a metaphor, and to explain the metaphor I will give the argument to show what I mean by this anchorage. But the anchorage is more fully explained in the other thesis. You wanted to have the fifth or the fourth? Which one? The fourth.

My fourth thesis is that the self, or full consciousness, is exercising a plastic control over some of our movements which, if so controlled, are human actions. Many expressive movements are not consciously controlled, nor are many movements which have been so well learned as to have sunk into the level of unconscious control. Now, I mentioned riding a bicycle amongst the movements which have been so well learned that they have sunk into the level of unconscious control. But I may perhaps add here something which is of interest: namely, if we have learned certain movements so that they have sunk below the level of conscious control, then if we try to follow them consciously we very often interfere with them so badly that we stop them. I call this the 'centipede effect' because there is a very nice story of the spider and the centipede. The spider says to the centipede, 'Look here, I have only eight legs. I can manage eight, but you have a hundred. I cannot imagine how it is that you know at each moment which of your hundred legs to move.' So the centipede said, 'It is very simple.' And he has been paralysed ever since. Now the centipede effect is a very real effect. The violinist Adolph Busch – perhaps some of you know his name, he died about twelve years ago and he was a friend of mine – he told me that he once played Beethoven's Violin Concerto in Zurich, and afterwards the violinist Huberman came and asked him how he played a certain passage. Busch said it was quite simple – and then found that he could no longer play the passage. The attempt to do it consciously interfered with his fingering, or whatever it was, and he could no longer play it. That is very interesting and actually shows the function of this process of becoming unconscious. Obviously it is a process by which we, as it were, clean the slate of consciousness, for the moment, in order to make it capable of following other things. That is to say, when you can play a thing on the violin so well that the fingering and everything connected with the technique of playing has sunk into the unconscious – or into the *physiology*, as I usually say – then you can concentrate on the presentation of the whole piece. You need not worry about it. You can have the whole piece in your mind and develop it with all its dramatic elements and without worrying about how to play it. And obviously that is the function – just as if you learn to drive a car well, and make the various movements and so on unconsciously, you can pay full attention to the traffic situation, which, of course, is much more important. So we can say in all these examples that the conscious control is the highest control, while the other controls sink into subconsciousness and unconsciousness. And we can also say that only the highest control remains a fully conscious action, so that we know what we are doing.

Questioner 2: We all use words like 'higher' and 'lower' and things like that. But I wonder why it is that an action which becomes explicitly conscious – a skill such as playing the violin, or anything else you'd like to mention – when a skill, which at some point has been very much of a conscious struggle, is mastered and then becomes part of the subconscious, so to speak, and becomes something we call a 'skill' – we call it a 'skill' because it is recognized as something that is done well – in what sense then is that *lower* than consciousness as we normally talk about it in common ordinary language? Because it seems to me when we move something out of that realm into explicitness, or what you call 'consciousness', it then becomes a fumbling problem.

Popper: It's lower in the sense of the hierarchy of control. About the control system: let us take, for example, a child having to learn how to balance itself. I do not have to pay any attention to balancing myself and can concentrate, for example, on talking to you. I need not worry about my balance. I can even lift my leg without losing my balance. Of course, lifting my leg is a conscious movement. But keeping my balance while I make this movement is unconscious. It is fairly clear that the general hierarchical character of animal control shows that these are really lower. That is to say, they are put *below* another control. Of course there is always a certain amount of interaction, especially if something goes wrong and they stumble, and so on, and the interaction becomes pretty violent, and it becomes a conscious action again. But it is more likely to be one of a series of controls at the same level, whilst the higher control is always unique – that is, the *highest* control. That is the centre, so to speak. That is really the thing. Of these lower controls, certain vague feelings may still always come up and interfere with these higher controls. For example, the violinist cannot concentrate only on the fingering of a piece of music – he must also manage his bow. I suppose Busch's problem was only a problem of fingering and not a problem of the right hand. Now, the left hand and the right hand, in the case of a violinist, have to be controlled independently, up to a point, because the movements are to a considerable extent independent. These will be *two* controls – more or less on the same level, but below the master control, the central control.

Questioner 2: Perhaps what I am suggesting is that perhaps – I don't know how you would do this schematically – I think I am suggesting that there ought to be . . . .

Popper: A kind of pyramid?

Questioner 2: Another level which ought to include skills. In other words, I would not put that on the second level, or even as interaction between the second and third levels. I would put skills on a fourth level.

Popper: You mean in this thing here?

> *World 3: theories, objective problems*
> *World 2: dispositions to behave*
> *World 1: physical states*

Of course, one can subdivide it. I do think that skills which have been mastered, in so far as they are incorporated in our physiology, belong to this second level. But the skill in the abstract – that is to say, the *rules* of the skill – belong, of course, explicitly to the third level. Take, for example, language. Now, my skill in the English language is very bad. But if anyone really masters the rules, then he need not think. It comes automatically. He does not know *how* he is talking. He does not consciously search for words and rules of grammar. He concentrates on the content of his talk, and it just runs along. But the rules which he follows belong to world 3. They are now incorporated in world 2, but you can make them explicit. And if you do make them explicit, then they belong to world 3. They belong to world 3 especially if you formulate them. But even so far as they cannot be formulated but are the object of learning, they belong to world 3. Of course, you *can* have further worlds. I have, for example, myself distinguished between 'aim structure' and 'skill structure'. The point is that all these things are, in a way, duplicated. That is to say, they belong to world 3, and can be understood and grasped in world 2, and incorporated in the second world in dispositions. Such duplications are very unfashionable. One of the

118

motives of modern philosophy is to avoid these duplications. It is a motive of positivism and of phenomenalism, as you probably know, to have just one word and not several words. One word representing another word, that is a *terrible* thing! They have just one word. But in reality, there is no doubt that these things are complicated. When a child learns a language it does not know – and never knows – the grammar as explicit rules. But, nevertheless, there *is* a grammar which it first incorporates by some sort of mixture of imitation and innate grasp, and then makes in the end a dispositional affair. But of course it is something *objective* which it incorporates in this way, and therefore it is something belonging to world 3. Is that sufficient? *Of course* you can distinguish. I am in that sense a pluralist, and I would never fight in favour of the theory that there are *only* three worlds. You can subdivide them as much as you like, and such subdivisions may for certain problems be quite important. But for oversimplification, I think these three are quite useful. I don't take it more seriously than that. I was once asked by a fairly famous symbolic logician – he suggested that before this theory of the three worlds can be taken seriously I should explain the concept of world 3 through an axiom system. But I don't take it as seriously as that at all. It is a metaphor which helps us to see certain relations. You can't axiomatize such things: they are signposts and nothing more. There are many things which cannot be put in axiomatic form.

Questioner 3: Would you accept the formulation that the function of consciousness is to consider alternatives, and that when behaviour involves the following of a pattern – however detailed or skilled – it works better when there are no alternatives to consider, if it is below the level of consciousness?

Popper: Yes, I would. Of course one has to say more about this, but that is the main thing. There are alternative possibilities. These alternative possibilities are tried out and their consequences are anticipated, and this anticipation then demands that we have some sort of imagination of these consequences. Very often all this goes very quickly. But we anticipate the consequences of the alternatives. The alternatives are no good if we do not anticipate the results, and in order to anticipate their results we have to have some sort of imagination. And I suppose imagination actually works more or less on a lower level in picture form. I don't think pictures are really necessary for consciousness, as we can see from blind people, who certainly do not have visual pictures as we have, but nevertheless may get through very well. But what is common to both blind and sighted people is that these consequences are represented at least by feelings of success or failure, pain or pleasure, or something like that, and then lead to the corresponding action. This seems to me to be the real point of the emergence of nearly full consciousness – not full consciousness yet, but something approaching it: namely, that we imagine the consequences of these alternatives. That is somehow or other an act of imagination, and there some decisive step is made towards full consciousness. That is what I suggest. And here we understand then that full consciousness may – even nearly full consciousness – may be biologically valuable and may, therefore, further develop. This theory is, of course, terribly vague and somewhat difficult, because it is quite obvious that we know nothing about lower stages of consciousness – about animal stages of consciousness.

All this has to be frightfully speculative. On the other hand, if we do not want to accept physicalism or behaviourism, which may be very convenient but certainly very false, we cannot help but see the body–mind problem in evolutionary terms. It's the only way in which we can somehow get near it. And if we see it in evolutionary terms, then I think it is clear that Descartes is better than Spinoza. Even if Spinoza is right, and even if electrons have their subjective states, it is not really what we are after. This kind of momentary consciousness is so far removed from what we are interested in that the problem of evolution certainly still exists. That is to say, the problem then is how do we get from the electron state of consciousness to the human state of consciousness? And that can only be explained by evolution. So even if we accept Spinoza's similar parallelistic theory, all the problems remain. They are no: really in any way solved. We will never know whether Spinoza is right or wrong. We will never know about the insight of electrons – actually, even the electrons do not know – because this kind of consciousness is ever so far removed from anything like subjective knowledge, if it exists at all.

I hope you understand the argument. If there is parallelism – if mind and body do run parallel – then connected consciousness would be a kind of memory, and this can be parallel only to a physical system which has a memory. Now many physical systems have memory. For example, magnets have memory. So physical systems pretty far removed from life have memory. Probably all crystals have memory, and magnets have memory because they are crystals, probably. It seems that all crystals have somehow a memory of their history. They are more fragile, since certain developmental events have happened in the making of the crystals and similar things. So we can speak of memory in a physical sense. And it is pretty clear that if parallelism is right, then memory in a subjective sense can at best emerge where there is memory in a physical sense, and therefore cannot emerge on the level of electrons or atoms – at best on a molecular level.

Questioner 4: Would your theory make it such that Freud's formulation of the Oedipus complex or the Oedipal theory signalled the end of the effect of the Oedipal complex in human life? In other words, your knowledge of Oedipal tendencies makes it such that we now take action against them, and this would mean that the third world has drastically affected the second and first worlds?

Popper: If you like. I would, however, put it very differently, because I am not a Freudian. I would say that Freud's theory has *terribly* affected world 2. I think Freud's theory is one of those false theories which, if they are believed in, become partially true. But whether you put it in this way or in your way, I would say that there is a very considerable effect on world 2 from psychoanalytic theory. In this, at any rate, we agree. I do think that by talking too much about sex we overemphasize it. The more it is talked about, the greater will be its role in life. This is some of the influence of the third world upon the second.

Questioner 5: Would you say we can speak of the self and full consciousness as the same for these purposes?

Popper: Yes.

Questioner 5: The self is dependent upon the third world, which is dependent upon language. And language is genetically based. But you also say in your second thesis that the self is dependent upon certain particular – well, there are certain theories in the third world, and you mentioned space, time, physical objects, and people, and so forth. But then you say in number 5 that we are not at the mercy of any particular third world theory. So now you would claim somehow that language as a general structure is genetically based, but that no particular objectification within language is genetically based, and all these are therefore learned....

Popper: Some perhaps. I should say that the idea of physical objects – that is to say, the idea of an external world with certain invariants in it – is most likely genetically based. Animals have it already, and have had it for ever so many millions of years. So it is likely to be genetically based. As we know, moving animals guard themselves against running against rocks. So they have a theory about that, and most likely this is genetically based. Some of these theories are genetically based. Take another example: we know that animals and plants have clocks built in, and there is therefore a genetically based *sense of time*. But also there is almost certainly no genetically based *theory* of time. By this I mean the following. Animals do not, so far as we know, see themselves extending through time into the past. They have memories, but the memories are just making them act differently. Or perhaps they have pictures turning up in dreams, or something like that. But they do not have a consciousness of themselves going back through time as we have in ourselves. In the idea of the self, this theory is innate. So this theory is probably not genetically based. But part of the theory of body seems to me to be genetically based.

Questioner 5: But what if that theory turns out to be false? Would it be possible for that theory to turn out to be false?

Popper: Yes, the theory is false if you throw a human being into the sea. He will try to get hold of something firm, but he will not be able to. Instinctively, he will try to snatch for something, but he will not be able to. And so the theory turns out to be false. There are no solids in the sea, and the genetically based theory of solids and the significance of solids will disappear for him. Similarly, of course, if you throw him into empty space, as we can do now. If you push him out into space in a space suit without training him, he will try to get hold of something firm, but he will certainly not succeed. So the theory is genetically based, but may turn out under certain situations to be false.

Questioner 5: And so we may be able to develop a plastic control? We may not ... ?

Popper: Of course the space traveller has already corrected the theory. And if he has been trained properly, then the correction will even become part of his dispositional outfit.

Questioner 6: And would that also entail accepting that if a mutation occurred which subtracted these genes from his constitution, that it would be retained?

Popper: We don't know what occurs in a mutation. Anything may occur in a mutation. A mutation may be lethal.

Questioner 6: But that mutation for which he has no use – that mutation which arises and subtracts the genetic material that he is no longer using, and in fact is trained against – is that mutation is more likely to be accepted?

Popper: That may be accepted. Anything may happen in a mutation, as I say. It may be positive, it may be negative. Some mutations may be more frequent than others. But anything may occur, and some may be good and some may be bad. Is that an answer? No? Then I have not quite understood your question.

Questioner 6: I am trying to visualize some of the effects which space travel and other unusual experiences could possibly have on human structure. And according to your theory, behaviour comes first and mutations follow suit. This would, perhaps, lead to a wide range of speculation. No?

Popper: No. You see I don't say that behaviour comes first and mutation follows suit. What I say is that the *selection* of mutation follows suit. A mutation may occur at *any* time. Mutations happen *all* the time. But the *selection* of mutation will be strongly dependent on the behaviour which has been adopted. You understand? So it is possible – thinkable – that when space travelling becomes more generally accepted, some mutation will be selected which would do away with our expectation of bodies. But much would have to happen before these would be selected. Space travel would have to become pretty universal before this kind of thing could make a genetic difference.

Questioner 7: There are some experiments currently being done by some physiologists and physicists where they are teaching rats to run a maze, and then killing the rats, taking out their brains, pulverizing them, and spinning out the RNA, and then injecting it into other rats. And they run the maze in the same fashion. How do you respond to this in terms of the kind of physicalism you were attacking earlier?

Popper: First of all, as you probably know, these experiments have been severely criticized. But let us assume they are right. It would mean that where I am speaking about sinking into the subconscious, this would correspond to the development of a chemical reaction. This is what these experiments would suggest. That is to say that if something sinks into the unconscious – I have said sinking into the physiology, now physiology may be chemistry – so I would not say this in any way affects my view. But I am a bit dubious about it. I don't think the experiments are quite unambiguous. But I would not be so very surprised, because somehow something must be the carrier of these learned patterns, and it may be the chemistry of the body just as well as anything else. Only if it is the chemistry – certain big molecules or whatever it is – only then could it be injected into other animals. Of course this is perfectly possible, but as I say – it started with these flatworm experiments ....

Questioner 7: I think it's a curiosity, and the experiment actually is the business of imprinting information, which is what these people are curious about. There is a physicist in the city doing this.

Popper: What shall I say? It may very well be that it is as simple as all that. It may also very well be that it is much more complicated than that, and that you cannot inject it. We don't know. It may be that these things are partly transferable in this way, or they are not.

Questioner 8: I would like a clarification of the meaning of 'aim structure', because there seem to be two meanings of the idea of an aim structure, one of which would be almost a duplication of a mutation, whereas the other is simply an absorption of the mutation itself. In the first case you have a departure from a system of behaviour, which would be almost – which would act at least in the same manner in which a mutation would act. And this seems to be more free. This sense of 'aim structure' seems to be more free. In the second case you have an absorption of a mutation in terms of an amelioration of the conditions, or of the environment itself, by any kind of improvement theory, such as survival of the fittest or other. Are these two senses of 'aim structure' compatible? Or are they more than compatible? Are they, perhaps, complementary?

Popper: If I understand you well, then what you want to distinguish is an aim structure which has been genetically entrenched from an aim structure which is only a kind of new behaviour. Let us take again my example of the woodpecker. I suppose that what has happened in the development of the woodpecker is that, for some reason or other, some problem has arisen, and in response to that problem the woodpecker has changed its taste for food. A new preference for a new kind of food has developed. Two things may happen now. This new preference may become genetically entrenched. That is to say, some mutations, probably with anatomical effects on the brain – I don't know, but something like that – may make a lasting change in the taste. The other possibility is that no such thing happens and only a broadening spectrum of possible behaviour takes place. That is to say, for a time this is preferred, but at a later time not. So there is the question of specialization or no specialization. If there *is* a specialization, then there is likelihood of this specialization being followed by an entrenchment – by a genetic entrenchment. This is the case where behaviour is the spearhead of a mutation. This is also the case, I think, where we could say that, although the animal may be extremely fit, it is likely not to survive drastic changes in the environment because of the entrenchment. If the situation leads more to a spread of possible behaviour – that is to say, to greater plasticity of the control – this is rather the opposite, namely making the animal likely to survive even fairly drastic changes. Is that more or less an answer to your question? So there are two possible changes in the aim structure, both beginning in the same way – namely, with a change of taste in this case – but the one may become genetically entrenched and the other may not. Now, I think it is very remarkable about man that, although language seems to be genetically entrenched, practically none of the exosomatic instruments which we have developed seems to be in the slightest way genetically entrenched. So, in that sense, language has actually led to a great spread of the possible behaviour roles, rather than to a narrowing of them. And this seems to me one of the decisive factors in human evolution. There does not seem to be a conceivable way in which language does harm to us, because what we are speaking about, and how we use it, is left open to us. But there are many conceivable ways in which language helps us. And especially, perhaps, it has prevented further entrenchment. I don't know how that is. At any rate, it has not led to further entrenchment.

Questioner 8: Isn't there anything between the aims which are guided by language and the aims which are, say, perhaps understood simply in terms of the enlargement of the plasticity of the controls? I am thinking of Mumford's theory of the machines being prior to language – Lewis Mumford speaking about the machines and saying that the machines are prior to language. I do not agree with him.

Popper: I think this is almost certainly false.

Questioner 8: Yes, but I was wondering how you would answer that particular thing? He would put the machines somewhere between the aims that are *guided* by language and the aims that are simple mutations or controlled *expansion*. And in between he would put . . . .

Popper: I think that everything speaks in favour of machines coming very late, especially when not even the simplest machine shows any sign of genetic entrenchment. That indicates that they come very late. So I think this theory is obviously false. And language is genetically entrenched, so it is probably much older than any machine. So we have first, probably, language. And with human descriptive language we have a tremendous evolution of imagination due to the possibility of story-telling. And from here I think we can now understand the possibility of a wide spectrum of tools, or machines if you call them so, which adjust themselves so completely differently to the environment. One of the most interesting cases of highly developed machines is that of the Eskimos. The tools of the Eskimos are extraordinarily specialized. An Eskimo's harpoon, an Eskimo's kayak – all of these are extremely complicated. A kayak is almost a submarine. It is possible to turn over in it, and be under the surface in it, and so on. All of this is extraordinarily developed. But, of course, nothing of it has a genetic basis. It is all traditional, and very different from the machines used by all other races, and very specialized for the particular environment in which the Eskimos live, and in which they have not lived for very long, for all we know. So this shows the plasticity of this field, and indicates that Mumford is wrong.

Questioner 8: I would suspect that, although he bases his arguments on empirical evidence, he is talking more as a matter of principle – perhaps because of a conviction that language itself can be instrumentalized, even instrumentalized at a most basic level, a theory that has also been advanced in other quarters.

Popper: Of course, I *also* think that language is instrumental. It is not *only* instrumental, but it *is* instrumental. That is to say, there is no doubt about the fact that theories are instrumental. The question of instrumentalism versus non-instrumentalism is not whether theories are instrumental, but whether they are *only* instrumental and nothing else. So I would agree here with the instrumental character of theories, but I would say they are something else also. Any further questions?

Questioner 5: I was going to ask you another question – it may be too trivial. I was going to ask you, on this scheme, how you would describe the interaction of these three levels in the business of a skilled physician diagnosing a problem.

Popper: You have actually a group of physicians coming tomorrow to the seminar, so we can perhaps discuss it there. But anyway, it is in this case particularly clear that the skill of the physician is very largely a world 3 affair. Almost completely, especially in diagnosis. Although a surgeon, for example, has it also in the skill of his fingers – so to speak, at his fingertips – and although even diagnosis may become, in some physicians, partly unconscious and almost instinctive. I know that there are some doctors who, as it were, in entering a room can 'smell' a diagnosis. They have a kind of feeling for it. But that is not so important. The really important thing is that diagnosis is almost entirely a skilled trial-and-error affair. That is to say, it is a trial-and-error affair which proceeds systematically – as many trial and errors do; by no means all are random – according to a plan which in itself has developed out of trial and error. The doctor has learned a kind of programme of the questions to be asked. There are some very general questions about age and so on to be asked, and then some specific questions about where the pain is felt and what is wrong with the patient, and so on. And by a kind of routine, certain things are excluded. It is in the main a matter of error elimination – a systematic error-elimination method which is learned from books or learned in the clinic. By a systematic trial-and-error method, and a special systematic error-elimination method, he then comes to a small number of possibilities. And from here on, the process is then, as a rule, again elimination of one possibility after another of the small number, let us say, by blood tests, or whatever it may be. And then remains the diagnosis. Now, of course, this all assumes that the human physiology is reasonably simple. That is to say, if it is not so simple as expected, then the diagnosis will be a mistake – which can happen. That is roughly the process. In this process, some of the methods of elimination themselves become almost dispositional, if they have been often done. Still, it is only world 3 which has led to the thing becoming dispositional – that is to say, world 3 together with the routine, like with a bicycle.

6

THE SELF,
RATIONALITY, AND
FREEDOM

Ladies and Gentlemen:

The topic of this lecture is The Self, Rationality, and Freedom. It is a vast topic, and the danger of degenerating into all kinds of vague generalizations is great, especially in a field in which so much is speculative.

I will first say a little more about the ego or the self than I could say in my last lecture, and then proceed to rationality.

First, about the self: my central thesis, as formulated in my last lecture, is that the self or the ego is anchored in world 3, and that it cannot exist without world 3.

Before discussing this thesis more fully it may be necessary to remove the following apparent difficulty. As I have here so often said, world 3 is, roughly, the universe of the products of our minds. But how can this be if, on the other hand, our minds, or our selves, cannot exist *without* world 3?

The answer to this apparent difficulty is very simple. Our selves, the higher functions of language, and world 3 have all evolved and emerged together, in constant interaction. Thus there is no special difficulty here. To be more specific, I deny that animals have states of full consciousness or that they have a conscious self. The self evolves together with the higher functions of language, the descriptive and the argumentative functions.

Animals have a highly developed spatial sense – a sense of orientation which, no doubt, is largely, if not completely, the unconscious result of instinct combined with the results of spatial exploration. Similarly, both animals and plants have inbuilt clocks, and thus a sense of time. They are, I conjecture, also conscious. But what they lack – all this is conjecture, of course – is the ability to see themselves as extending in time and space and as acting in time and space. So far as they are conscious, their consciousness is directed by their inner states on to significant events outside themselves – if not exclusively, then almost exclusively.

My theory of animal anticipation: they anticipate movements of an enemy or prey – frog and fly – by a template effect, by a partial innervation of responding movements, which makes the final innervation quicker and more appropriate. These partial innervations are, I conjecture with Gomperz and James/Lange, represented in feelings.

As opposed to this, full consciousness of self contains, as one of its components, a knowledge of ourselves stretching back in time, at least for some short distance. And our sense of location in space contains at least a sketchy history of how we came to the place in which we are located. If we wake up in a strange place, we are liable to ask ourselves, 'Where am I? Have I had an accident? How did I come here?'

But we do not live only with an at least rudimentary consciousness of our past history, but also with an at least rudimentary consciousness of our expectations, which normally involve our aims and purposes, our immediate and our more remote interests in life.

All this is present in us in a dispositional form. But these dispositions are dispositions to recall the past to our consciousness. They are thus very different from the equally dispositional spatio-temporal sense of animals. For the human dispositions mentioned are linked with other dispositions directed towards theories: a theory of time based upon the circle of day and night, a theory of space as an ordered set of invariable spatial distances between prominent physical bodies, and a theory of physical bodies as the prominent invariants in our environment. But what constitutes our selves or our egos is, in part, that we can see our selves located in this frame and as having reached our locations through movements in it. Moreover, we see our bodies as invariants, like other bodies, or, perhaps, as slowly changing. And we realize and understand the cycle of being awake and being asleep, and the interruptions to our consciousness in sleep, while our bodies continue to be there. Now all this is, clearly, of a *theoretical* character: *it depends upon descriptive language, and even on argumentative language.*

An important part is played in all this by the specifically human functions of our memory.

Memory, in the widest sense, may be ascribed to a thing whose behaviour depends upon its history. In this widest sense, magnets and, more generally, crystals, and thus most complex physical structures – and certainly all organisms – may be said to have memory. As I mentioned in my previous lecture, electrons have no memory. Nor, for all we know, have atoms. From the behaviour of a sleeping dog, we may conjecture that all dogs dream. And bits and pieces of memory are likely to play in these dreams a role similar to that in our own dreams. But the controlled recall of a human experience, such as when we have learned a poem by heart years ago and consciously try to recall it, is made possible only through our links with world 3 objects. This holds even for the conscious recall of past events: they are found by trying to connect them with other bits and pieces of memory according to some theory we hold about our past history. In all this, we use knowledge which is linguistically formulated – at least in part, or dispositionally.

From all this it is clear that even the role played by memory in our conscious self is anchored in world 3, the world of criticizable knowledge, of knowledge in the objective sense. We constantly criticize our attempts to recall or reconstruct some memory as deficient, and we try to find the missing elements.

Thus we arrive at the result mentioned in my last lecture: the ego or self is closely linked with our higher functions of language. And this suggests that full consciousness interacts with the speech centre of our brain.

I will now formulate some of these ideas, and also some additional ideas, in the form of three theses.

1   In the evolution of the *species*, the ego or the self or self-consciousness emerges together with the higher functions of language – that is, the descriptive and the argumentative functions – and it interacts with these functions.

2   In the development of the *child*, the ego or self or self-consciousness develops with the higher functions of language, and therefore after the child has learned to express himself, and to communicate with other persons, and to understand his relations to other persons, and to adjust himself to his physical environment.

3   The self or the ego is linked with the central control function of the brain on the one hand, and it interacts with world 3 objects on the other. In so far as it interacts with the brain, the location of interaction may be anatomically localizable. I suggest that

the interaction is centred in the speech centre of the brain.

On the first of these theses, concerning the linguistic evolution of the species, I have said quite a lot before, and I shall not add anything new.

On the second thesis, concerning the development of self-consciousness in the child, I will make just one or two remarks.

I am a great admirer of, and believer in, common sense. But common sense is sometimes seriously mistaken. It is so in connection with the theory of knowledge, as we have seen. For the common-sense theory of knowledge is subjectivist and sensualist. The common-sense theory of knowledge is the bucket theory of the mind which asserts that, as a matter of our personal histories, we – and 'we' means the various selves – acquire knowledge through our senses.

This theory was taken over by the idealist philosophers. The solipsistic philosophy and the philosophy of Berkeley – usually called 'subjective idealism' – which I mentioned in my preceding lecture, spring from this mistaken theory of knowledge. They believe that all knowledge consists of my experiences, or of my memories of some of my experiences.

But if we speak of my experiences, then the ego or self comes in. Thus, all these philosophies take the ego or the self or the subject for granted, and they then try to construct the external world – including other persons and other minds – on the basis of the ego or of the content of our mind. And they fail.

But as a matter of psychological fact, the dispositional knowledge of the ego or self comes later in the development of the child than the dispositional knowledge of the external world and of other persons and other minds. For the dispositional knowledge of the self is acquired during that process of growth in which we acquire descriptive and argumentative language. The development of the child is parallel to the evolution of the species: while the dispositional knowledge of the external world and of other persons is accessible to animals, the self emerges only on the human level.

I will now comment on my anatomical conjecture. This conjecture seems to be testable, and the tests are fascinating and, indeed, staggering. When I first developed this anatomical conjecture I was unaware that experiments had been going on for some time which could be interpreted as tests of my conjecture. (I first read about these experiments in Sir John Eccles' Eddington Lecture in 1966.)

I shall very briefly report these experiments.

Our brain consists of two symmetrical halves, the left half serving the right side of the body, and vice versa. In most people – at any rate, in the vast majority of right-handed people – the speech centre is located in the left hemisphere of the brain.

The two halves of the brain are linked by a kind of bridge carrying a huge number of connections between the two cerebral hemispheres. This bridge is called 'the great cerebral commissure'.

Now in some surgical operations on the brain, this bridge is cut right through, and the connection between the left- and right-hand sides is severed.

The operation was first performed on animals, including primates, and it was noticed that they were perfectly happy afterwards – and so are the human patients on whom it has been performed during the last four or five years.

Incidentally, the operation is performed on people suffering from severe epileptic attacks, and it appears to be a real cure for epilepsy. The people on whom the operation was performed are happy, and they behave in every way like ordinary people, though under investigation differences may be detected.

I want now to report briefly on a few of these differences.

Operated people can read as well as ever with both eyes or with the right eye.

But now comes the interesting thing. As long as an operated man cannot control, by organs on the right-hand side of his body, such as his eyes or hands, what his left hand is doing, he is unconscious of the movements of his left arm and hand. He is not a split personality – he is a complete personality, but fully conscious only of those signals which the left half of his brain receives from the right half of his body.

For example, an operated man used to smoke cigarettes and to reach for the cigarette with his left hand, to put it into the left corner of his mouth, and to use a lighter with his left hand to light it. He did so after the operation quite normally, even if he could not see with his right eye what he was doing. But in this case, he was unconscious of what he was doing, that is, he was unable to give proper replies to questions about his movements. Yet if he puts the cigarette into the right corner of his mouth, he will know this and say so.

Generally, as long as his right side is not involved, he can give no account of his left-sided reactions, and he declares that he does not know that he has made any movements. These movements remain unconscious, because they are not referred to the speech centre.

With this, I conclude my very perfunctory survey of a new theory of the self, or consciousness, and its main function, which is to establish a kind of remote and very plastic control of our speech centre through world 3. I shall now proceed to some remarks on human rationality.

I am a rationalist. That is, I am trying to stress the importance of rationality for man. But like all thinking rationalists, I do not assert that man *is* rational. On the contrary, it is obvious that even the most rational of men are in many respects highly irrational. Rationality is not a property of men, nor a fact about men. It is a *task for men to achieve* – a difficult and a severely limited task. It is difficult to achieve rationality even partially.

I never quarrel about words, and I never define words, but I have to explain what I mean by 'rationality'. I mean by 'rationality' simply a critical attitude towards problems – the readiness to learn from our mistakes, and the attitude of consciously searching for our mistakes and for our prejudices. Thus, I mean by 'rationality' the attitude of conscious, critical, error elimination.

Now it is not merely the fact that this attitude is difficult to achieve which sets important limits to our rationality. Nor is it the fact that we are not so much rational animals as passionate animals. All that is obvious. The really important fact is this. All criticism must be piecemeal – even what may appear to us in science as a revolutionary criticism which rejects, and reconstructs, a dominant scientific theory.

The reason for this is very simple. Criticism can only be criticism of some tentative theory which we have formulated and put before us as an object to be investigated and criticized – as we investigate, for example, a watch that we may wish to buy for a birthday present.

Yet our knowledge consists of a huge amount of dispositions, expectations, and theories of which only a small number can be placed consciously before us at a particular moment of time. In fact, at any moment there will be only one theory before us which is selected for criticism, only one theory under investigation. But a huge amount of knowledge, knowledge on all kinds of levels of importance, is *used*, mostly unconsciously, in the investigation of any theory. I have called this knowledge 'background knowledge'. It is *used* in the investigation, and thus it is uncritically accepted, or taken for granted, during the investigation.

This does not mean that the investigator is, in any way, obliged to take the whole of this background knowledge uncritically for granted. It may occur to him that a mistake is hidden not in the theory under investigation, but in some elements of the background knowledge. And thus, he may criticize a *piece* of the background knowledge. But this piece then ceases to be background knowledge, and becomes knowledge under investigation.

Here, the most interesting example is, perhaps, Einstein, who investigated certain difficulties in Maxwell's theory of the electro-magnetic interaction of moving bodies and found that he could solve his problems by challenging the tacit background assumption, never before noticed, that simultaneity is an absolute concept. Einstein showed that, and why, simultaneity has to be referred to a so-called 'inertial frame' of all bodies which are at rest within this frame – or, in other words, that simultaneity of distant events is transitive only within such a frame. Before Einstein, we assumed that if an event A is simultaneous with B, and B with C, then A is always simultaneous with C. Einstein showed that this holds for distant events only if A and B, on the one hand, and B and C, on the other, are simultaneous *within the same inertial frame*. This highly sophisticated correction had to be made, according to Einstein, to an apparently obvious and never before explicitly formulated assumption belonging to what I call 'background knowledge'. This correction had revolutionary significance. And the example may be used to illustrate the impossi-bility of criticizing all our knowledge at one time.

It is a challenge to our ingenuity, to our critical imagination, to discover which element of our knowledge – possibly of our background knowledge – is to be blamed for any particular difficulty or discrepancy which has arisen in connection with a problem or a theory. Our tentative conjectures are always risky and often daring, and to propose that we should critically investigate a so far unsuspected – and perhaps even unconscious – assumption may in itself be a new and daring conjecture.

Since most of our subjective knowledge is inborn, or traditional – and thus dispositional – it is also not explicitly formulated. Some of this background knowledge may even be built into the grammar of our language – and, therefore, like the air we breathe, constantly assumed or presupposed in our arguments, so that it is difficult for us to detect it and to criticize it. This, indeed, was the case with simultaneity. For the grammar of all phrases constructed with the words 'the same' – such as 'at the same time', or 'of the same length' – implies transitivity. What Einstein showed was, in effect, that this usage, combined with any method of establishing the simultaneity of distant events in a frame, leads to the conclusion that any event – say, the Inauguration of President Johnson – is simultaneous with any other event – say, the Inauguration of President Nixon – which is absurd. The usage is all right, however, so long as it is applied in ordinary life, since we live in an approximately inertial system.

All this shows that our criticism can be only piecemeal, and thus that there are some limitations to our rationality – that is, to the scope of our criticism. However, the following important statement seems to hold.

> While our criticism cannot tackle more than one or two problems or theories at a time – and should try to tackle, preferably, only one – there is no problem or theory or prejudice or element of our background knowledge that is immune to being made the object of our critical consideration.

Thus, rationality has inherent limitations only in the sense that these considerations prevent a headlong rush into a general criticism of everything at the same time. But there are, on the other hand, no limits to the objects of our rational criticism. Nothing is exempt from coming under critical scrutiny, at one time or another.

From all this, it may be seen that we are far from being rational. We are fallible not only in all we think we know but even in our critical approach. We have to *select* problems and theories for rational criticism. But this act of selection is, in itself, a tentative conjecture. And so we may easily spend a lifetime on the wrong problem: this is one of the reasons why we are fallible even in our critical approach.

The revolutionary idea – once formulated by Plato – that we should clean the whole canvas, that we should wipe clean our slate of knowledge and begin afresh from the beginning, is not feasible. If we were to start again where Adam started, there is no earthly reason why we should do any better than Adam did, or get any further. But even Adam did not start with a clean slate. So we should have to jettison all the expectations and prejudices, all the dispositional knowledge acquired during evolution. We should have to return not to Adam, but to the beasts, to the animals, and, indeed, to the amoebae. Thus the dream of canvas cleaning is not too revolutionary or progressive, but retrogressive and even reactionary. We have to be modest, and conscious of our fallibility, and we should remember the bold yet always tentative advance by which life conquers new environmental conditions and creates new worlds by tentative steps. In this way we emancipated ourselves from the semi-conscious world of the animals. In this way we have achieved *full consciousness*. In this way we have invented science. And in this way we have proceeded in science, getting nearer and nearer to the truth.

This may be the place to make a few critical remarks about what I call 'the myth of the framework'.

What I call 'the myth of the framework' is a view, widely held and often even unconsciously accepted, that all rational argument must always proceed within a framework of assumptions – so that the framework itself is always beyond rational argument. One could also call this view 'relativism', for it implies that every assertion is to be taken as relative to a framework of assumptions.

A fairly common form of the myth of the framework also holds that all discussions or confrontations between people who have adopted different frameworks are vain and pointless, since every rational discussion can operate only within some given framework of assumptions.

I regard the prevalence of this myth as one of the great intellectual evils of our time. It undermines the unity of mankind, since it dogmatically asserts that there can, in general, be no rational or critical discussion except between men who hold almost identical views. And it sees all men, so far as they try to be rational, as caught in a prison of beliefs which are irrational, because they are, in principle, not subject to critical discussion. There can be few myths which are more destructive. For the alternative to critical discussion is violence and war – just as the only alternative to violence and war is critical discussion.

The main point, however, is that the myth of the framework is simply mistaken. Admittedly, a discussion between people who hold identical, or almost identical, views is bound to proceed more easily than a discussion between people who hold strongly opposed, or vastly different, views. But only in the latter case is the discussion likely to produce something *interesting*. The discussion will be difficult, but all that is needed is patience, time, and good will on both sides. And even if no agreement is reached, both sides will emerge from the discussion wiser than they entered it. By 'good will' I mean here the admission, to start with, that we may be wrong, and that we may learn something from the other fellow. The myth of the framework may be regarded as a sophisticated form of a point of view called 'justificationism' – that is, the doctrine that rationality consists in the rational justification of our beliefs, or, in objective terms, the rational justification of our theories. But justificationism is a logically impossible doctrine. There simply can be no rational justification of our theories.

As we have seen, all theories are guesses or conjectures, and all that we can rationally justify is a tentative *preference* for one or two of the competing theories. But there is all the world of difference between the justification of a *preference* – for the time being – for one of the competing theories, and the justification of a *theory*. To justify a theory is to show that it is true. But we may justify a preference, even for a false theory, if we can show that of all the competing theories it appears to come nearer to the truth than any of the others.

I have explained my view of justificationism and what I have put in its stead. The myth of the framework also rejects justificationism, but it is less radical in its rejection. It retains more of justificationism than I do, for it says that justifications have to be relativized to a framework which, in its turn, cannot be justified.

As against this, I contend that, even if we admit the doctrine of a framework, we would have to stress that the various frameworks can compete. This means, as in the case of theories, that those who defend one framework can criticize another. And we, the spectators as it were, may try to form a rational judgement as to which framework produces the best criticism of the others, and as to which can be most successfully defended against the criticisms which proceed from the others. In fact, there is no difference in principle between a framework and a theory.

It has sometimes been asserted that the different frameworks of assumptions are just as different as different languages, and that those brought up in different frameworks simply do not understand each other, so that rational criticism is impossible. This view has been supported by reference to Benjamin Lee Whorf's study of the language of the Hopi Indians. But the important thing is that Benjamin Lee Whorf *did* learn to speak Hopi, and I have met Hopi Indians myself who spoke English much better than I do. In other words, every human language can be mastered by a sufficiently gifted outsider.

Exactly the same holds for a framework of assumptions. It can be studied, understood, and criticized by an outsider. This makes it possible for frameworks to compete.

What we may learn from all this can perhaps be expressed as follows. In every moment of our mental growth we are, as it were, imprisoned in a framework and in a language. The framework and the language severely limit our thinking. Yet this is an imprisonment in a Pickwickian sense: for at any moment we are free to break out of the prison by criticizing our framework and by adopting a wider and truer framework and a richer and less prejudiced language.

This breaking out of our framework may be difficult. But it is possible. And it may be engendered or stimulated by the clash with another framework – that is, by confrontation. Nothing can be more fruitful. In fact, the history of civilization shows how fertile such a culture clash can be. Our own western civilization is the result of a number of culture clashes, such as the many clashes between the Greek and oriental cultures. The story of one of these clashes is told by Homer, and that of another by Herodotus, and both were highly conscious of the significance of the events. These early clashes contributed to the emergence of Greek science and of Greek rationalism – that is, to the emergence of the Greek love of rational critical discussion.

So much for the myth of the framework.

And now some final words on rationality.

As I indicated before, we are always the prisoners of our prejudices, or of our framework of assumptions. But we can, with the help of the world 3 method of putting our theories and our assumptions outside us – of formulating them clearly, so that they can be criticized – always break out of this prison through rational criticism.

There is no question that we possess this freedom. Our relation to world 3 cannot be understood without it. When we are faced with a world 3 object, such as a theory, our first task is to understand it. But understanding a theory does not mean accepting it. Nor does it mean that we regard it as the best of the competing theories. In fact, before we can form a judgement concerning the preferability of one theory over some other theories, we must first understand them *all*.

Understanding a theory has many degrees. The lowest degree of understanding is to understand all the words and the sentences from a linguistic point of view. Thus you might say of a book, or of a lecture, 'I understood every word of it.' Sometimes you may continue, 'But although I understood every word of it, I have not the slightest idea what it is all about.' In order to understand what a theory is about, we have first to understand the *problems* which the theory tries to solve. And you have to understand the various ways which have been tried in order to solve these problems – that is, the various competing theories. For without these, you cannot understand, in a fuller sense, any of them, since understanding, in this fuller sense, means appreciation, or appraisal. And, of course, there are still higher degrees of understanding, such as finding out for yourself where the difficulties of the various theories lie – that is, the new problems P_2 to which they give rise – and how these difficulties can be met. There is no end to this, since every theory gives rise, at the very least, to the problem of whether the theory cannot be explained in its turn by some higher level theory. For no theory is an ultimate explanation.

All this shows that our appraisal of a theory cannot be determined simply by logic or by its structure, unless, perhaps, the theory is obviously false or makes obviously false claims – to completeness or finality, for example – like the theories of physicalism and parallelism that I discussed in my lecture last week. All this means that there is a tremendous range of freedom in our relationship with world 3, in our understanding, and in our appraisal of theories. And there is still more freedom if we consider human creativity.

My main thesis was that all selves are anchored in world 3. But the way we are thus anchored admits of a wide range of possibilities. We explore and we add to world 3 in almost all things we do. And this means not only freedom but a great responsibility.

I will end by discussing the relationship between a man and his work – a thing which is of the greatest importance for all of us.

According to the theory of self-expression, the quality of the work we do depends upon how good we are. It depends only on our talents, on our psychological, and, perhaps, on our physiological states. I regard this as a false, vicious, and depressing theory. According to the theory of world 3, there is no such simple relationship. There is, on the contrary, a give-and-take interaction between a person and his work. You can do your work, and, thereby, grow through your work so as to do better work – and grow again through *that* better work, and so on.

There is a constant feedback through which world 3 acts upon us. And the most active part of world 3 in this is our own work, the product which we contribute to world 3. This feedback can be greatly amplified by conscious self-criticism. The incredible thing about life, evolution, and mental growth is just this method of give and take, this interaction between our actions and their results by which we constantly transcend ourselves, our talents, and our gifts.

This self-transcendence is the most striking and important fact of all life and all evolution, and especially of human evolution. It is contained in the move from P_1 to P_2.

In its prehuman stages it is, of course, less obvious. And so it may indeed be mistaken for something like self-expression. But on the human level, self-transcendence can be overlooked only by a real effort. As happens with our children, so with our theories: theories tend to become largely independent of their parents. And as may happen with our children, so with our theories: we may gain from them a greater amount of knowledge than we originally put into them.

The process of learning – of the growth of subjective knowledge – is always fundamentally the same. It is *imaginative criticism*. This is how we transcend our local and temporal environment by trying to think of circumstances *beyond* our experience: by trying to find, construct, invent, and anticipate new situations – that is, *test* situations, *critical* situations – and by trying to locate, detect, and challenge our prejudices and habitual assumptions.

This is how we lift ourselves by our bootstraps out of the morass of our ignorance – how we throw a rope into the air and then climb up it, should it get any purchase, however precarious, on any little twig.

What makes our efforts differ from those of an animal or of an amoeba is only that our rope may get a hold in the world 3 of critical discussion: the world of language and objective knowledge. This makes it possible for us to discard some of our competing theories. So if we are lucky we may succeed in surviving some of our mistaken theories – and most of them are mistaken – while the amoeba will perish with its theory, its belief, and its habits.

Seen in this light, life is exploration and discovery – the discovery of new facts, of new possibilities, by way of trying out possibilities conceived in our imagination. On the human level, this trying out is done almost entirely in world 3. We do it by our more or less successful attempts to represent, in the theories of this third world, our first and second worlds. And we do it by trying to get nearer to the truth – to a fuller, a more complete, a more interesting, logically stronger, and more relevant truth – relevant, of course, to our problems.

What I have called 'world 2' – the world of the mind – becomes, on the human level, more and more the link between world 1 and world 3. All of our actions in world 1 are influenced by our world 2 grasp of world 3. This is why it is impossible to understand the human mind and the human self without understanding world 3. And it is also why it is impossible to interpret either world 3 as a mere expression of world 2, or world 2 as the mere reflection of world 3.

The process of self-transcendence through mutual growth and feedback is something that can be achieved in all walks of life and in all fields. It is possible for us to achieve it in our personal relations. It may not depend only on us, and it may lead to disappointments. But disappointments are met with in all phases of life. Our task is never to give way to a feeling that we did not receive what was our due. For as long as we live, we always receive more than is our due. To realize this, we have only to learn that there is nothing that the world owes us.

We all can participate in the heritage of man. We all can help to preserve it. And we all can make our own modest contribution to it. We must not ask for more.

EDITOR'S AFTERWORD

Knowledge and the Body–Mind Problem is based upon the Kenan Lectures that Sir Karl delivered at Emory University in the spring of 1969. These lectures were given without notes, and this book owes its existence, at least in part, to the tape recordings that were made of them and of the discussions that followed them. These tape recordings were transcribed, apparently, in the early 1970s. Sir Karl then began to revise the lectures, and he even wrote a preface, apparently intending to rework them into a book. Several versions of each lecture were prepared and criticisms were solicited and received. But the work apparently did not go too far before the pressure of other commitments forced Sir Karl to put the manuscript aside. It lay in his drawer until 1986, when the Hoover Institution on War, Revolution and Peace acquired Popper's papers and created The Karl Popper Archives at their library in Stanford University.

The text published here differs both from the Kenan Lectures as they were delivered at Emory University and from the typescripts that I found in the Popper Archives. So while this book is based upon the Kenan Lectures, it is not intended to be an historical record of them. On the contrary, the typescripts that I found were already an extensive revision of the original lectures. And what is published here is an extensive revision of what I found. Most of the revisions that I have made have been stylistic in nature and designed to smooth the transition from an oral to a written text. Others have been more substantive. And I have, in a few places, been forced to reconstruct text where the original recordings failed. Sir Karl has encouraged me to make these revisions, and, in particular, to simplify his expression whenever it was possible to do so without altering his thought. I have not indicated any of my revisions in the text, so as not to distract the reader's attention. And since Sir Karl has approved them as his own, I see no reason to indicate them here. I do, however, want to thank Sir Karl for trusting me with his work, and especially for the many stimulating conversations that we have had concerning it.

Knowledge and the Body–Mind Problem is the second volume to be published from The Karl Popper Archives. It is the first that consists of previously unpublished material. And I want to acknowledge with gratitude the work that W.W. Bartley III, and The Hoover Institution on War, Revolution and Peace devoted to the creation of these archives.

In March of 1992 the Ianus Foundation began financial support of my work in the Popper Archives. Since then, it has supplied me with a microfilm copy of the archives and the equipment necessary to use it. And it has also made possible an extensive transatlantic telephone tutorial with Sir Karl. I want to thank the Scientific Director of the Ianus Foundation, Werner Baumgartner, for his vision of a Popper tree, and, most of all, for his friendship. And I want to thank the President of the Ianus Foundation, Jim Baer, who made sure that I had the best possible equipment for the job. I also want to thank Elisabeth Erdman-Visser (who first suggested to Sir Karl that I edit his work), Ursula Lindner and Melitta Mew (each of whom provided necessary moral support), Raymond Mew (who read the manuscript and made many helpful suggestions), Richard Stoneman (Senior Editor at Routledge), Sue Bilton (who guided the book through its publication with Routledge), and Victoria Peters (who helped her do it). In January of 1994, the Soros Foundation and the Central European University assumed financial support of my work. I want to thank George Soros for his interest in this project, and for his commitment to Sir Karl's vision of the world as an open society. As I mentioned earlier, this volume was first planned for publication in the 1970s. Jeremy Shearmur worked on it then, and I owe a great debt of gratitude to him, since his work has undoubtedly made mine easier. Finally, I owe more than I can say to Kira Victorova, my colleague and my wife, who is, in many ways, the co-editor of this book.

M.A. Notturno
Chicago, 1994

BIBLIOGRAPHY

The following is a list of Karl Popper's books in the English language

The Open Society and Its Enemies, Volume I: The Spell of Plato, Routledge & Kegan Paul, London, 1945, revised 1952, 1957, 1962, 1966.

The Open Society and Its Enemies, Volume II: The High Tide of Prophecy: Hegel, Marx, and the Aftermath, Routledge & Kegan Paul, London, 1945, revised 1952, 1957, 1962, 1966.

The Poverty of Historicism, Routledge & Kegan Paul, London, 1957.

The Logic of Scientific Discovery, Hutchinson, London, 1959; reprinted by Routledge, London, 1992. Translation of Logik der Forschung, Julius Springer, Vienna, 1934; revised edition J.C.B. Mohr, Tübingen, 1989.

Conjectures and Refutations: The Growth of Scientific Knowledge, Routledge & Kegan Paul, London, 1963, revised 1965, 1969, 1972, 1989.

Objective Knowledge: An Evolutionary Approach, Clarendon Press, Oxford, 1972, revised 1983.

Unended Quest: An Intellectual Autobiography, Open Court, La Salle, Illinois, 1982; revised edition published by Routledge, London, 1992. First published as Autobiography of Karl Popper in The Library of Living Philosophers, ed. Paul Arthur Schilpp, Open Court, La Salle, Illinois, 1974.

The Self and its Brain: An Argument for Interactionism, with John C. Eccles, Springer Verlag, Berlin, Heidelberg, and London, 1977; Routledge & Kegan Paul, London, 1983.

The Open Universe: An Argument for Indeterminism, Volume II of the Postscript to The Logic of Scientific Discovery, ed. W.W. Bartley, III, Hutchinson, London, 1982; paperback published by Routledge, London, 1988.

Quantum Theory and the Schism in Physics, Volume II of the Postscript to The Logic of Scientific Discovery, ed. W.W. Bartley, III, Rowman & Littlefield, Totowa, New Jersey, 1983; Unwin Hyman, London, 1982; reprinted by Routledge, London, 1992.

A Pocket Popper, ed. David Miller, Fontana, London, 1983; republished as Popper Selections, Princeton University Press, Princeton, New Jersey, 1985.

A World of Propensities, Thoemmes, Bristol, 1990.

BIBLIOGRAPHY

In Search of a Better World: Lectures and Essays from Thirty Years, Routledge, London, 1992. Translation of *Auf der Suche nach einer besseren Welt*, Piper, Munich, 1984, 1988.

The Myth of the Framework, ed. M.A. Notturno, Routledge, London, 1994.

Knowledge and the Body–Mind Problem, ed. M.A. Notturno, Routledge, London, 1994.

NAME INDEX

SUBJECT INDEX

theories, die in our stead
decoding 5, 6, 112, 113, 142; as
genetically based 112 (*see also*
language, genetic basis of)
definitions: vs derivation 33 (*see also*
language, two sides of); vs
explanation 18, 19, 54, 104;
Tarski's definition of truth *see*
truth, Tarski's definition of
demarcation, problem of
(positivism) 76
description 100, 101; objective vs
subjective 98, 99; true 49, 86,
102, 104
diagnosis 127
discovery 141; vs invention 48 (*see
also* world 3, autonomy of); of
problems 35, 75, 110; of
solutions 35, 38; in world 3 20,
27–31, 35, 36, 42, 45, 46, 48
discussion: critical 11–13, 25, 79, 98,
137, 141; as the only alternative
to violence and war 137
dispositions 13–15, 24, 34, 81–4, 90,
110, 118, 130, 131, 134; acquired
14; inborn 14, 15, 25, 44, 45, 112,
122, 135; to learn 15, 44, 45, 84,
88, 119 (*see also* language,
learning); mental 95
dogs 87, 88, 100, 111, 131
dreams 70, 71, 106–8, 111, 122, 131;
see also consciousness, degrees of
dualism 8, 52, 109; Cartesian 5, 109

ecological niche 66, 67, 70, 83
ecology 66
ego *see* self
electrons 74, 109, 110, 131
emotional: response 85–8, 98, 112,
113, 130 (*see also*
communication; functions of
language, communicative); states
81
energy *see* matter and energy
environment 39, 56–9, 66, 67, 69, 73,
83, 113; change in 12, 38, 54, 58,
61–3, 71, 72, 137
epiphenomenalism 110, 111
epistemology 4

error elimination 10–12, 55, 56, 58,
60, 63, 64, 79, 134; *see also* trial,
and error elimination
Eskimos 126
ethics 99, 100; emotive theory of
(C.L. Stevenson) 99; as
man-made 45, 46
eugenics 54
evolution 34, 54, 55, 59, 69, 70, 80,
90, 141; biological 10, 12, 32, 40,
73, 81; emergent 39, 48, 53, 58,
62, 63, 65, 68, 71, 79, 80, 105,
112, 115, 129, 131; of human
language *see* language, evolution
of human; of human mind 10, 90,
120, 129; of science *see* science,
evolution of; of the species 131,
132; theory of 48, 52, 57, 79, 81
(*see also* Darwinism); of world 3
10, 12, 22, 25, 33, 38, 48, 112, 129
evolutionary: ascent 49, 53, 54, 61,
62, 66; tree 55, 57, 68
expectations 14, 15, 24, 89, 112, 113,
119, 123, 130, 134, 136, 141; *see
also* communication, as release of
expectations
experience 13, 25, 131, 132, 141
explanation: no theory is an
ultimate 140; *see also* definitions,
vs explanation; theories,
explanatory

facts *see* propositions,
correspondence with facts
falsehood 108; criteria of 97
feedback 114, 115, 140, 142
first world *see* world 1
flatworms 124
flies 130
food 112, 113, 125; *see also*
preference, for a certain food
forms *see* concepts, deified Platonic
'fourth realm': of norms 17; of skills
118
framework *see* myth of the
framework; theories
freedom 9, 129, 139, 140
frogs 130
functions of language 48, 81–93, 99,

129–31; argumentative, or critical 39, 84, 87, 88, 90–2, 98, 99, 129–32 (*see also* story-telling); Bühler's theory of the 84–6, 99; command 85; communicative 84–8, 93–5, 98, 99 (*see also* communication); descriptive, or informative 81, 82, 84, 86–94, 98, 99, 129–32 (*see also* description); expressive 81, 84–8, 93–5, 98, 99 (*see also* art, as self-expression); hierarchy of 84–92, 98, 99, 129

galaxy 65
genetic: ascent *see* evolutionary, ascent; basis of behaviour *see* behaviour, genetic basis of; engineering 54, 123; patterns 63, 79 (*see also* specialization, as genetic trait); tree *see* evolutionary, tree; types 56
geometry 26–9, 35–7, 40, 45, 48; autonomy of 26, 29, 35, 36; invention of 26, 27, 29; as man-made 26, 35
grammar 88, 89, 92, 118, 119, 135, 136; of music 95; rules of 119
Greeks 37, 45, 74
guesses *see* conjectures; hypotheses

Hamlet 5, 6, 21, 22, 23
harmony 74, 75
Hebrew culture 45
hereditary trait *see* specialization, as genetic trait
heredity 56, 59–61; and mutability 52–4
Hopi Indians 138
hypnosis 111
hypotheses 10, 33, 97, 138

idealism 108, 132; subjective *see* solipsism
imagination 15, 81, 89, 113, 119, 120, 141; critical 135; evolution of 126
imitation *see* specialization, as tradition

individuals 12, 55, 56, 58–61, 63, 79, 80; breeding of 79; as spearheads 56, 63
industrialization 12
inertial frame 135, 136
infection: communicative 85, 88; of planets *see* planets
instinctive behaviour 22, 83, 99, 129
instrumentalism 17, 126, 127; *see also* theories, as instruments
instruments 126; as exosomatic organs 13, 34, 82, 83, 89, 90, 100, 101, 125
intellect 15
intelligence 108
intention 9, 17, 32, 43; understanding of 29
interaction, body–mind *see* body–mind, interaction (*see also* speech centre); between consciousness and unconsciousness 117; electromagnetic interaction of moving bodies 135; location of 109, 115, 131, 132 (*see also* pineal gland; speech centre); between man and his work *see* work, man learns from his; between physical and mental states 5, 109, 114; between the self and its brain 115, 131; between selves, higher functions of language, and world 3 129, 131; as a sufficient criterion of reality 17, 47 (*see also* world 3, reality of); between the three worlds 5, 7, 8, 21, 41, 43, 44, 46, 110, 115, 127, 142 (*see also* work, man learns from his); between two minds 27, 99
intuition (Plato) 49
invention 81–2; *see also* discovery; products, of human minds
Ionian School 92
irrefutability 107, 108

justificationism 138

Kepler's laws 74–5, 78; Hegel's

the theory of 49–52; and
language learning *see* language,
learning; logical relations within
40–1, 42; as man-made 33, 37, 40,
44, 52; memory anchored in 131;
Plato's 49–50; of products of
human mind 19, 22, 24–7, 30, 31,
33, 47, 95, 129; reality of 17, 20,
33, 47, 50, 51, 52 (*see also*
interaction, as a sufficient
criterion of reality); role of 29;
self anchored in 129, 134; and

story-telling 82 (*see also*
story-telling; theories,
explanatory); survival value of
10, 16, 38; as timeless 29, 36; as
world of theories and arguments
33, 49, 114, 115, 121
worlds: distinguished by Plato
49–50; interaction between *see*
interaction, between the three
worlds; more than three can be
distinguished 17, 25, 118, 119
(*see also* norms)